THE BEST OF AMERICAN HERITAGE
THE CIVIL WAR

Edwin S. Grosvenor

AMERICAN HERITAGE • NEW WORD CITY

Published by New Word City, Inc.

For more information about New Word City, visit our Web site at
NewWordCity.com

PROLOGUE

For some Americans, the Civil War may seem like ancient history, a jumble of half-remembered events – the bombardment of Fort Sumter, Pickett's Charge at Gettysburg, Abraham Lincoln's Emancipation Proclamation and his assassination by John Wilkes Booth.

But the Civil War was an enormous and profound event that challenged the very existence of the United States. The attempt of Southern slave states to secede from the Union, coming only two generations after the nation's founding, posed a critical test of the United States' character, endurance, and will to survive. Oliver Jensen, one of *American Heritage*'s editors, wrote that the Civil War is "America's most monumental drama and morality tale." And within that larger drama were innumerable first-hand stories of courage, cunning, and loss. "Civil War armies were the most literate that ever fought a war up to that time," writes historian James McPherson, while "twentieth-century armies censored soldiers' mail and discouraged diary keeping. Thus we have an unparalleled view of the Civil War by the people who experienced it."

Lincoln saw the Civil War as God's punishment of North and South alike for the sin of slavery. If that were so, the penalty was severe. More than 600,000 Americans lost their lives, millions were maimed or had their property stolen or destroyed. Atlanta, Charleston, Columbia, and Richmond, along with countless small towns, were left in ruins.

So it's not surprising that given its outsized importance in our nation's history, the Civil War has always occupied an important place in the pages of *American Heritage*. One of the most acclaimed historians of the war, Bruce Catton, was the magazine's founding editor. Catton attracted many other writers who also had insights and details to share about the Civil War.

As Catton's term as editor neared its end, David McCullough joined the staff. McCullough's talent is evident in this volume's wonderful portrait of Harriet Beecher Stowe and the creation of *Uncle Tom's Cabin*. When Stowe's novel appeared in 1852, only a small minority of the country opposed slavery despite years of debate over the Fugitive Slave laws and the moral arguments of abolitionists. Stowe's book changed the way the country thought and talked about slavery. In it, she humanized the plight of slaves. Within a year of publication, *Uncle Tom's Cabin* sold more than 500,000 copies. Although Stowe wasn't a crusader, she "had written the abolitionist's manifesto," wrote McCullough. Senator Charles Sumner and many others credited the book with rousing the public to action and bringing about the election of Abraham Lincoln. Frederick Douglass praised the novel as "a flash to light a million camp fires in front of the embattled hosts of slavery." Lincoln reportedly remarked that "this is the little woman who started the war," when Stowe visited the White House a few years later.

Ever since the Civil War, observers have wondered if better political leadership could have averted the bloodshed and destruction and whether slavery would have collapsed on its own. In another chapter in the pages ahead, Columbia University historian Allan Nevins argues that the succession of three weak presidents between 1850 and 1861: Millard Fillmore, Franklin Pierce, and James Buchanan, who one contemporary called "the damndest old fool that has ever occupied the presidential chair," could have contributed to the advent of the war. Could stronger and cannier leaders have somehow avoided the debacle? "The greatest mistake a nation can make," Nevins warns, "is to put at its helm an unprincipled man so pliable that he will palter with a clean-cut and momentous issue."

Certainly, one event that sped the nation's movement to war was John Brown's extraordinary attack on Harpers Ferry. In this volume, Thomas Fleming tells the story of the raid, the flawed trial that followed, and the hanging of the raiders. Fleming describes how, on October 16, 1859, Brown and twenty-one armed followers seized the federal arsenal at Harpers Ferry and converted it into a fortress. Brown believed that slaves in the surrounding area would run away from their owners to join his group - then he could declare his own Virginia government and lead a force of blacks and whites into the South, freeing more slaves along the way.

But, fearful of brutal reprisal from their owners, slaves failed to turn up at Harpers Ferry, and the next day, a Virginia militia drove Brown and his band out of the arsenal and into the adjacent fire-engine house. A firefight raged for a day and a half until all but seven of the raiders were killed, captured, or had fled.

Their exploits, as well as those of less revered military leaders, are brought alive in this book. Included here is Stephen Sears's detailed and balanced portrait of Robert E. Lee. Sears writes that when a general asked one of Jefferson Davis's aides if he thought Lee had the ability to lead an army, he replied that "Lee is audacity personified . . . His name is audacity."

Sears also paints a very different, but equally powerful, portrait of George B. McClellan, whose reluctance to engage in battle arguably prolonged the war for years and cost countless lives. "McClellan seemed to be a strong, decisive commander, a general with an unmatched gift for organizing and motivating his troops," observes Sears. "But in battle, he was all but paralyzed by a loss of will and a fear of defeat."

Another lesser-known general, George Henry Thomas, gets his due in these pages. Peter Andrews describes how Thomas, "The Rock of Chickamauga" and the strategist behind Northern victories in the Western theater, was crucial to the Union's success.

In "Antietam," Bruce Catton describes in vivid detail the fateful day in September 1862 - the bloodiest day in American history – when the war turned in favor of the North. "In the entirety of the American Civil War, no single day was bloodier or more costly than that one day on the hills and fields overlooking Antietam Creek in western Maryland." A total of 22,717 lives were lost on this day.

The pages ahead are filled with vivid, sometimes quirky accounts of lesser-known characters, including the story of Belle Boyd, the glamorous

Southern spy, and war correspondent G. W. Smalley. One chapter describes the miraculously speedy construction of the North's ironclad warship, the USS *Monitor*, just in time to defeat the Confederate CSS *Virginia* and prevent Britain from siding with the South. Another illuminates the horrors of prison camps on both sides, highlighting the infamous Andersonville in Georgia.

R. N. Current tells us of the debate, even as the war's slaughter continued, over Lincoln's plan to rebuild the shattered nation – evoking another question: Could a leader different from Andrew Johnson have prevented the worst excesses of Reconstruction?

The end of the war prompted the greatest parade in the nation's history, with the North's two victorious armies marching through Washington to the tireless cheers of its grateful citizens. Before that, however, came the tragedy that would shape the country's course for a century to come: the assassination of Abraham Lincoln, reported in detail here by historian Philip B. Kunhardt, Jr.

The Civil War tested us as a nation like no other moment in our history, and the stories of heroism, folly, and suffering make for fascinating reading.

- Edwin S. Grosvenor

INTRODUCTION

"Americans just can't get enough of the Civil War," says Terry Winschel, historian of the Vicksburg National Military Park. Millions of visitors come to Vicksburg every year. Tens of thousands of Civil War re-enactors spend hundreds of dollars on replica weapons, uniforms, and equipment; many travel long distances to help restage Civil War battles. Another 250,000 Americans describe themselves as Civil War buffs or "hobbyists."

As a beneficiary of this popular interest in the Civil War, I am often asked to explain what accounts for it - in particular, to explain my contribution to the literature on the war and its causes. *Battle Cry of Freedom*, was on national bestseller lists for several months as a hardcover book in 1988 and again as a paperback in 1989.

First, the human cost of the Civil War was by far the most devastating in America's history. The 620,000 Union and Confederate soldiers who lost their lives almost equaled the 680,000 American soldiers who died in all the other wars this country has fought combined. When we add the unknown but probably substantial number of civilian deaths - from disease, malnutrition, exposure, or injury - among the hundreds of thousands of refugees in the Confederacy, the toll of Civil War dead may exceed war deaths in all the rest of American history. Consider the Battle of Antietam, America's single bloodiest day. The 25,000 casualties there were nearly four times the number of American casualties on D-Day. The 6,500 men killed in one day near Sharpsburg were nearly double the number of Americans killed in combat in all the rest of the country's nineteenth-century wars combined.

As Thomas Hardy once put it, "War makes rattling good history; but Peace is poor reading." The sound of drum and trumpet, the call to arms, the clashing of armies have stirred the blood of nations throughout history. As the horrors and the seamy side of a war recede into the past, the romance and honor and glory forge into the foreground. Of no war has this been truer than of the Civil War.

William Faulkner said the past isn't dead; it isn't even past. As any reader of Faulkner's novels knows, the Civil War is central to that past that is present; it is the watershed of American Southern history; it is, as Mark Twain put it a century ago after a tour through the South, "what A.D. is elsewhere; they date from it." The symbols of that past-in-present surround Southerners as they grow up, from the Robert E. Lee Elementary School or Jefferson Davis High School they attend to the Confederate soldier enshrined in bronze or granite in their town square. Some of those symbols remain controversial and provoke as much passion today as in 1863: the song "Dixie," for example, and the Confederate flag, which for many Southern whites continue to represent courage, honor, or defiance while to blacks they represent racism and oppression.

This suggests the most important reason for the enduring fascination with the Civil War: Great issues were at stake, issues about which Americans were willing to fight and die, issues whose resolution transformed and redefined the United States.

The Civil War was fought mainly by volunteer soldiers. The Union and Confederate armies mobilized as volunteers a larger percentage of their societies' manpower than any other war in American history - probably in world history. Most of the volunteers knew what they were fighting for, and why. What were they fighting for?

If asked to define it in a single word, many soldiers on both sides would have answered: liberty. They fought for the heritage of freedom bequeathed to them by the Founding Fathers. North and South alike wrapped themselves in the mantle of 1776. But the two sides interpreted that heritage in opposite ways.

When Abraham Lincoln won the presidency in 1860 on a platform of excluding slavery from the territories, Southerners compared him to George III and declared their independence from "oppressive Yankee rule." "The same spirit of freedom and independence that impelled our Fathers to the separation from the British Government," proclaimed secessionists, would impel the "liberty loving people of the South" to separation from the United States. One Georgia secessionist declared that Southerners would be "either slaves in the Union or freemen out of it." Men from Texas to Virginia rushed to enlist in this "Holy Cause of Liberty and Independence" and to raise "the standard of Liberty and Equality for white men" against "our Abolition enemies who are pledged to prostrate the white freemen of the South down to equality with negroes." From "the high and solemn motive of defending and protecting the rights which our fathers bequeathed to us," declared Jefferson Davis at the outset of war, let us "renew such sacrifices as our fathers made to the holy cause of constitutional liberty."

But most Northerners ridiculed Southern professions to be fighting for the ideals of the American Revolution. That was "a libel upon the whole character and conduct of the men of '76," said the antislavery poet and journalist William Cullen Bryant. The Founding Fathers, he argued, had fought "to establish the rights of man . . . and principles of universal liberty." The South, insisted Bryant, had seceded "not in the interest of general humanity, but of a domestic despotism . . . Their motto is not liberty, but slavery." Northerners did not deny the right of revolution in principle; after all, the United States was founded on that right. But "the right of revolution," wrote Lincoln in 1861, "is never a legal right. . . . At most, it is but a moral right, when exercised for a morally justifiable cause. When exercised without such a cause revolution is no right, but simply a wicked exercise of physical power." In Lincoln's judgment secession was just such a wicked exercise. The event that precipitated it was Lincoln's election by a constitutional majority. As Northerners saw it, the Southern states, having controlled the country's government for the previous two generations decided to leave the Union because they lost an election.

For Lincoln and the Northern people, it was the Union that represented the ideals of 1776. They believed that the republic established by the Founding Fathers was a fragile experiment in a world bestridden by kings, emperors, czars, and dictators. Most republics through history had eventually been overthrown. Republics in Latin America came and went with bewildering rapidity. The United States in 1861 represented, in Lincoln's words, "the last, best hope" for the survival of republican liberties in the world. "Our popular government has often been called an experiment," Lincoln told Congress on July 4, 1861. But if the Confederacy succeeded in splitting the country, it would destroy the experiment. "The central idea pervading this struggle," said Lincoln, "is the necessity . . . of proving that popular government is not an absurdity. We must settle this question now, whether, in a free government, the minority have the right to break up the government whenever they choose."

Many soldiers who enlisted in the Union army felt the same way. A Missourian joined up as "a duty I owe my country and to my children to do what I can to preserve this government as I shudder to think what is ahead of them if this government should be overthrown." A New England soldier wrote to his wife: "I know . . . how great a debt we owe to those who went before us through the blood and sufferings of the Revolution. And I am willing - perfectly willing - to lay down all my joys in this life, to help maintain this government, and to pay that debt."

Freedom for the slaves was not part of the liberty for which the North fought in 1861. That was not because the Lincoln administration supported slavery; quite the contrary. Slavery was "an unqualified evil to the negro, to the white man . . . and to the State," said Lincoln on many occasions in words that expressed the sentiments of a Northern majority. "The monstrous injustice of slavery . . . deprives our republican example of its just influence in the world - enables the enemies of free institutions, with plausibility, to taunt us as hypocrites." Yet in his first inaugural address, Lincoln declared that he had "no purpose, directly or indirectly, to interfere with . . . slavery in the States where it exists."

Lincoln was bound by a constitution that protected slavery in any state where citizens wanted it. The republic of liberty for whose preservation the North was fighting had been a republic in which slavery was legal everywhere in 1776. That was the great American paradox - a land of freedom based on slavery. Even in 1861, four states that remained loyal to the Union were slave states, and the Democratic minority in free states opposed any move to make the war for the Union a war against slavery.

But as the war went on, slaves took the first step toward making it a war against their plight. Coming into Union lines by the thousands, they voted with their feet for freedom. As enemy property, they could be confiscated by Union forces as "contraband of war." This was the thin edge of the wedge that finally broke the American paradox. By 1863, a series of congressional acts plus Lincoln's Emancipation Proclamation enlarged Union war aims. The North fought not just to ensure that the nation born in 1776 "shall not perish from the earth," but to give that nation "a new birth of freedom."

Northern victory in the Civil War resolved two fundamental issues left unresolved by the Revolution: whether this fragile republican experiment called the United States would survive and whether the house divided would continue to endure half slave and half free. Many doubted the republic's survival; many European conservatives predicted its demise; some Americans advocated the right of secession and periodically threatened to invoke it; eleven states did invoke it in 1860 and 1861. But since 1865 no state or region has threatened secession, not even during the "massive resistance" to desegregation from 1954 to 1964. Before 1865, the United States was the largest slaveholding country in the world.

In the process of preserving the Union, the Civil War also transformed it. Before 1861 the words United States were a plural noun: "The United States are a large country." Since 1865, United States has been a singular noun. The North went to war to preserve the Union; it created a nation. This transformation can be traced in Lincoln's wartime addresses. His first inaugural address contained the word Union twenty times and the word nation not once. In Lincoln's first message to Congress, on July 4, 1861, he said Union forty-nine times and nation only three times. In his 1862 public letter to Horace Greeley concerning slavery and the war, Lincoln spoke of the Union nine times and the nation not at all. But in the Gettysburg Address fifteen months later, he did not refer to the Union at all but used the word nation five times. And in the second inaugural address, Lincoln spoke of one side's seeking to dissolve the Union and the other side's accepting the challenge of war to preserve the nation. The decentralized Republic, in which the post office was the only agency of national government that touched the average citizen, was transformed by the crucible of war into a centralized polity that taxed people directly and created an internal revenue bureau to collect the taxes, expanded the jurisdiction of federal courts, created a national currency and a federally chartered banking system, and drafted men into the Army.

From 1789 to 1861 a Southern slaveholder was president of the United States two-thirds of the time, and two-thirds of the Speakers of the House and presidents pro tem of the Senate had also been Southerners. Twenty of the thirty-five Supreme Court justices during that period were from the

South. A century passed before another resident of a Southern state was elected president. For half a century after the war hardly any Southerners served as Speaker of the House or president pro tem of the Senate, and only nine of the thirty Supreme Court justices appointed during that half-century were Southerners. For better or for worse, the flames of Civil War forged the framework of modern America.

- James M. McPherson

1
"THE LITTLE WOMAN WHO MADE THIS BIG WAR"
– DAVID MCCULLOUGH

H arriet Beecher Stowe was brought up to make herself useful, and it suited her.

As a child, she was known as Hattie. She was cheerful but shy, prone to fantasies, playful, and pretty. Years later, she described herself differently: "To begin, then, I am a little bit of a woman - somewhat more than forty, about as thin and dry as a pinch of snuff; never very much to look at in my best days, and looking like a used-up article now." She wasn't altogether serious, but the description was one people remembered. It was in striking contrast to the huge reputation she gained when her *Uncle Tom's Cabin* swept the nation, bolstering the abolitionist cause and pitting North against South. Meeting her for the first time, Abraham Lincoln looked down from his six-foot-four height and said, "So this is the little woman who made this big war." It was only a minor exaggeration.

She was born in Litchfield, Connecticut in 1811, when Lincoln was two years old, and Dolley Madison was in the White House. She was the seventh of nine children of Roxana Foote and Lyman Beecher. Hattie was such a good worker, even when small, that her preacher father liked to say he would gladly have given $100 if she could have been born a boy.

When Hattie was young, she found most of her father's Calvinist sermons about as intelligible as the Choctaw language, she wrote later, and never was at peace with his religion. She still loved him though, and for all his gloomy talk of sin and damnation, it is not hard to understand why. He was a powerful, assertive figure who had an almost fiendish zest for life - for hunting and fishing with his sons, listening to music, and playing the violin, which he did badly. If he could only play what he heard inside his head, he told them all, he could be another Paganini. Best of all, he loved to "snare souls." Lyman Beecher needed to use all his tremendous energy. He kept a pile of sand in his cellar, and if his day was not enough to use him up or stormy weather kept him from outdoor exercise, down the stairs he would go to shovel sand.

On Sunday mornings, Lyman would bound along through the sunshine, late again for that appointed hour when, weekly, he brought down Calvinist thunder upon the heads of upright Litchfield people. He reserved a special wrath for drunkards and Unitarians, and he believed passionately in the Second Coming, although something made him shy away from the strictest tenet of his creed - total predestination and its logic. Once, when he agreed to exchange pulpits with another pastor, he was told that the arrangement had been preordained. "Is that so?" he said. "Then I won't do it!" And he didn't.

The happiest times in her childhood, Hattie wrote later, were days spent away from her father, visiting her Aunt Harriet in Nut Plains, Connecticut. Her aunt's house was filled with books and pictures gathered by a seafaring uncle and a wonderful old Tory grandmother, who in private still said Episcopal prayers for the king and queen.

At twelve, Hattie was a bit of a romantic. She often wandered off from the noisy parsonage to lie on a green hillside, gaze into the sky and dream of Lord Byron, the English poet. One month, she read *Ivanhoe* seven times.

In 1832, when Hattie turned twenty-one, Lyman Beecher answered the call to become the first president of the Lane Theological Seminary in Cincinnati, Ohio. He packed up his family and set off for what he called "the majestic West." He envisioned a New Jerusalem established on the banks of the Ohio River. The family spirits were lifted, and crossing the Allegheny Mountains, they sang "Jubilee." A Philadelphia journal likened the exodus of the Reverend Mr. Beecher and his family to the migration of Jacob and his sons.

The following summer, the man who was hired as Lane Theological Seminary's first professor, Biblical scholar Calvin Ellis Stowe, traveled west in the Beechers' wake. Accompanying him was his bride, Eliza, who became Hattie's best friend in Cincinnati but died shortly after her arrival. Apparently, shared grief over Eliza brought Hattie and Stowe together. Years later, with some of the proceeds from *Uncle Tom's Cabin*, they commissioned an artist to paint a portrait of Eliza, and every year after that, on Eliza's birthday, the two of them sat before the painting and reminisced about her.

Calvin and Hattie's wedding took place in early January, 1836. The night before the ceremony, trying to describe her emotions in a letter to a school friend, twenty-four-year-old Hattie confessed she felt "nothing at all."

Calvin was thirty-three, but he seemed as old as her father. He was fluent in French, German, Greek, Hebrew, and Italian; he was an authority on education; he knew the Bible better than her father did. He was said to have a grand sense of humor, but he was fat, forgetful, and fussy. In the midst of a crisis, Hattie discovered, he tended to take to his bed, demonstrating absolutely no "faculty," that Yankee virtue she defined as being the opposite of shiftlessness.

Calvin also had an eye for pretty women and a taste for spirits, but these proclivities, it seems, never got him into any particular trouble.

There was more. Calvin maintained that he was haunted by phantoms. They visited him most anytime, but favored dusk. They appeared quite effortlessly out of the woodwork, the floor, or the furniture. There was a regular cast of characters, Calvin said, as real and familiar to him as anyone else he knew, including a giant Indian woman and a dwarf who, between them, carried a huge bass fiddle. There was a troupe of Puritans from his native Natick in Massachusetts, shadowy and dark blue in color, and one "very pleasant-looking human face" he called Harvey. They performed music for Calvin Stowe, and somehow or other, they talked to him without making any sound at all, or so he said. He had no reluctance to discuss the subject, and there is no indication that any of his circle thought less of him for it.

The Stowes' marriage proved difficult from its start. Hattie became pregnant about the same time the state of Ohio requested that Calvin go to Prussia to study educational systems there. Professing a profound fear of sea travel, Calvin told Hattie he would never see her again in this life. She insisted he go anyway and bore their twin daughters while he was gone.

Calvin returned to Cincinnati after some months. A third child was born two years later, then another, and another, and two more after that. A professor's wages were never enough for the growing family, even when Lyman could pay Calvin in full, which was seldom. Hattie's health began to fail. "She lived overmuch in her emotions," one son explained years later.

"It is a dark, sloppy, rainy, muddy disagreeable day," she wrote to Calvin when he was in Detroit attending a church convention. "I am sick of the smell of sour milk, and sour meat, and sour everything, and then the clothes *will* not dry, and no wet thing does, and everything smells mouldy; and altogether I feel as if I never wanted to eat again."

She began taking increasingly lengthy trips to visit relatives, leaving Calvin and the children behind. She went to the White Mountains, then to Brattleboro, Vermont, to try the water cure. Gifts from admirers of the family paid her expenses. Hattie stayed in Brattleboro for nearly a year, living on brown bread and milk, enduring interminable baths, and writing exuberant letters to her family about moonlight snowball fights. No sooner did she return to the house in Cincinnati than Calvin decamped to Brattleboro, where he stayed even longer than she had. When a cholera epidemic broke out in Cincinnati and more than 100 people a day were dying, she came down with it, too - but wrote to tell Calvin to stay in Vermont.

Calvin and Hattie spent more than three years apart, and their letters speak of strong, troubled feelings. Stowe complained that Hattie never folded his newspaper properly and that her letters were too uninteresting for him to read aloud to his friends. She, in turn, ran on about her own troubles: The house depressed her. She worried about money. She hated the climate in Cincinnati. She thought too much about death.

Nevertheless, she told him, "There are a thousand favorite subjects on which I could talk with you better than anyone else. If you were not already my dearly loved husband, I should certainly fall in love with you."

Calvin responded in kind when she visited her sister in Hartford: "And now my dear wife, I want you to come home as quick as you can. The fact is I cannot live without you and if we were not so prodigious poor I would come for you at once. There is no woman like you in this wide world."

In the same letter, Calvin proclaimed to her - and apparently he was the first to do so - "My dear, you must be a literary woman. It is so written in the book of fate." He advised her to make all her plans accordingly, as though she had little else to do. "Get a good stock of health and brush up your mind," he prescribed. He also told her to drop her middle initial, E (for Elizabeth), from her name. "It only incumbers it and interferes with the flow and euphony." Instead, "Write yourself fully and always Harriet Beecher Stowe, which is a name euphonious, flowing, and full of meaning."

She had already written quite a bit: temperance tracts, articles on keeping the Sabbath, New England "sketches" from which she drew on Calvin's inexhaustible supply of childhood reminiscences. Once, she wrote an article about a slave. She sold these pieces to *Godey's Lady's Book* and other magazines for $2 a page on average, which was more profitable than taking in boarders, she decided. Other than Calvin, though, no one in her family took her writing seriously.

Harriet worked at her kitchen table with a baby in a clothes basket at her feet. She couldn't spell well, and her punctuation was a puzzle to her publishers. She dreamed, she said in a letter to Calvin, of a place to work without "the constant falling of soot and coal dust on everything in the room."

Calvin was traveling again in July 1849. Harriet wrote to tell him that their infant son Charley had died from cholera, the disease she had contracted the summer before. She had been unable to help the child, who suffered for almost a week.

Calvin returned, determined to leave Cincinnati. He accepted a professorship at Bowdoin College in Brunswick, Maine, and he sent Harriet and three of the children north ahead of him.

Stowe left Cincinnati in the early spring of 1850, a shabby little figure, perfectly erect, perhaps no more than five feet tall, nearly forty and pregnant again. She boarded a riverboat and made her farewells. She felt she was going home. But she was also heading for a notoriety of a kind known by few Americans before or since.

She sailed up the Ohio River to Pittsburgh, where she transferred to a canal boat. At Johnstown, the Allegheny Portage Railroad hoisted the boat and its passengers up and over the Allegheny Mountains. East of the mountains, Harriet traveled by rail to New York, crossing by ferry into Brooklyn to visit her younger brother, Henry Ward Beecher, pastor of Plymouth Church.

A few days later, she and the children went to Hartford. Her spirits were soaring. At Hartford, she stayed with her sisters Mary and Isabella, and in Boston, with her brother Edward. From Boston, Harriet took the Bath Steamer to Maine, sailing headlong into a nor'easter. On the day she and her children arrived in Brunswick, one story goes, the president of Bowdoin sent a professor named Smith down to greet the new faculty wife. Smith, however, returned disappointed, saying she must have been delayed. Nobody got off the boat, he said, except an old Irish woman and her brats.

Brunswick offered precious few of the eastern civilities Stowe desired. In fact, the house Calvin had taken in advance turned out to be "deserted," "dreary," and "damp." Industrious as ever, she went to work, refinishing floors, putting up wallpaper - the pioneer once again. Upon receiving a letter from Calvin in Cincinnati, stating he was dying and the family would soon be plunged into debt, Harriet read the letter with practical humor and burned it in the stove.

Calvin, still very much alive, showed up before summer when another of Harriet's babies was born. She rested two weeks. Even with Calvin's new professorship, which paid $1,700 a year, the Stowe family struggled financially. When winter arrived, Harriet's shoes were full of holes, and the house was so cold that the children sometimes had trouble sitting still long enough to eat their meals.

The following spring, Harriet began writing *Uncle Tom's Cabin or Life among the Lowly*. She wrote passionately about the evils of slaveholders and the humanity of slaves. On this subject, she joined her brother Edward, who grew ever more militant over the slavery issue.

The subject of the book had been all around Stowe for a long time. Lyman had made Litchfield farmers weep when he preached on the evils of slavery. In Cincinnati, Harriet had opened a Sunday school for black children, and the Lane Seminary had been a hotbed of abolitionist fervor. The Underground Railroad, she later claimed, went directly through her Cincinnati house. That was a bit of an exaggeration, but on one occasion, Calvin and her brother Charles did help a black woman and her child elude a slave hunter. The only time she was in a slave state, during a visit to Kentucky, she showed no particular emotion about it. However, stories she heard from the black women she knew in Cincinnati moved her, particularly those told by Eliza Buck, who helped Harriet with housework. Stowe was incredulous to learn that all of Eliza's children had been fathered by her former master in Kentucky.

Eliza told Harriet of lashings and of enslaved families split up and "sold down the river." Once on an Ohio River wharf, Stowe had seen with her own eyes a husband and wife torn apart by a slave trader.

During her stay in Boston en route to Maine, Harriet and her brother Edward had talked about the Fugitive Slave Bill under debate in Congress, which made it a federal crime to harbor or assist the escaped "property" of a slave master. Taking their conversation to heart, her duty was plain.

There was, she said, a standard higher than an act of Congress.

She did some research in Boston and corresponded with Frederick Douglass on certain details, but for all that, *Uncle Tom's Cabin* was written more out of something within her, something she knew herself about bondage and the craving for liberation than from any documentary sources or personal investigation of slavery in the South. Indeed, Harriet really knew little about slavery.

Edward's wife may have provided the encouragement Harriet needed to start writing the novel. "Hattie," wrote her sister-in-law from Boston, "if I could use the pen as you can, I would write something that will make this whole nation feel what an accursed thing slavery is." Harriet replied, "As long as the baby sleeps with me nights, I can't do much at anything, but I will do it at last. I will write that thing if I live."

It took Stowe a year to write *Uncle Tom's Cabin*. She wrote Uncle Tom's death scene first and in a single sitting, using brown wrapping paper when her writing paper ran out. The story appeared first in serial form in the antislavery newspaper *National Era* beginning in June 1851. The finished novel was published by John P. Jewett in two volumes on March 20, 1852.

Calvin thought the book had little importance.

He wept over it, but he wept over most of what Harriet wrote. Her publisher warned that her subject was unpopular and said she took too long to tell her story. On the advice of a friend who had not read the manuscript, she decided to take a 10 percent royalty on every copy sold rather than a fifty-fifty division of profit, which Jewett had also offered to her.

Harriet herself expected to make no money from the book; she thought it inadequate and was sure her friends would be disappointed with her. Much to her surprise, within a week of the book's release, 10,000 copies were sold. Jewett had three presses running twenty-four hours a day to keep up with demand. In a year, sales in the United States came to more than 300,000 copies. In England, where Stowe had no copyright and therefore received no royalties, sales were even higher. A million and a half copies sold in a year's time. The book was reprinted in thirty-seven different languages. "It is no longer permissible to those who can read not to have read it," wrote George Sand from France. Sand said Stowe had no talent, only genius, and called her a saint.

Uncle Tom's Cabin had a strange power over almost everyone who read it. People tried to interpret the book and explain how and why she wrote it. Harriet was not much help. At first, she said she really didn't write it at all, rather that the book came to her through visions and all she did was write down what she saw. When someone reproached her for letting the character Little Eva die, she answered, "Why, I could not help it. I felt as badly as anyone could! It was like a death in my own family, and it affected me so deeply that I could not write a word for two weeks after her death." Years later, she stated categorically, "God wrote it," and a great many of her readers were quite willing to let it go at that.

Uncle Tom's Cabin described the business of slave ownership in human terms. No writer had done that before. Slavery was argued over in the abstract, preached against as a moral issue, and whispered about in polite company. Stowe's book, however, made people *feel* what slavery was about. Moreover, she had made a black man her protagonist. She took his race seriously, and no American writer had done that before.

Harriet fervently believed that all citizens of the United States should take responsibility for the system of slavery. Every white American was guilty, the Northerner no less than the slaveholder, especially the church-going kind. Simon Legree, remember, was a Vermonter.

Stowe would have been heartbroken to learn that Uncle Tom would one day be used as a term of derision. For her, he was a black Christ figure. Uncle Tom is the one character in all her book who lives according to the Christian ideal. That she saw emancipation for the black man as a chance for dignity is evident in her plotline regarding Eliza's resolute, confident husband, George Harris. When George and his family, having escaped into Ohio, are cornered by slave hunters, George is prepared to kill his tormentors and die himself rather than allow his wife and son to be taken back into slavery. "I am a free man, standing on God's free soil," George shouts, "and my wife and my child I claim as mine. We have arms to defend ourselves, and we mean to do it. You can come up if you like, but the first one of you that comes within the range of our bullets is a dead man, and the next, and the next, and so on till the last."

Stowe seemed to be everywhere at once after her book was published – Boston, Brooklyn, Hartford, New Haven. Almost immediately, the South began boiling with indignation. She was a radical, they said. She began receiving threatening letters, and once, Calvin unwrapped a parcel addressed to her and found a human ear that had been severed from the head of a slave. Calvin became increasingly concerned about Harriet's safety. The Stowe family moved again, this time to Andover, Massachusetts, where Calvin took a teaching job at the local seminary.

Then they sailed to England, where huge crowds waited for Harriet at railroad stations. Hymns were composed in her honor, and children came up to her carriage with flowers. She traveled wearing a gray cloak and carried a paint box. She was a tireless tourist. In addition, she worried: "The power of fictitious writing, for good as well as evil is a thing which ought most seriously to be reflected on. No one can fail to see that in our day it is becoming a very great agency."

When the Civil War began, many people told Stowe it was *her* war, and she thought so, too. In South Carolina, the wife of a plantation owner wrote in her diary that slavery had to end, but added, "Yes, how I envy those saintly Yankee women, in their clean cool New England homes, writing to make their fortunes and to shame us."

Harriet Stowe never saw the Civil War as anything but a war to end slavery, and she quickly abandoned her Beecher pacifist principles. "Better, a thousand times better, open, manly, energetic war, than cowardly and treacherous peace," she said. Her eldest son, Frederick, enlisted in the Union army. Impatient with Lincoln for not announcing emancipation quickly enough, she traveled to Washington when he finally proclaimed that the South's slaves would be free, and met the president in the White House. He disarmed her with his now-famous greeting.

On January 1, 1863, the day the Emancipation Proclamation became effective, Harriet was attending a concert at Boston Music Hall. When an announcement of the historic event was made from the stage, someone called out that Stowe was in the gallery. The audience gave her a standing ovation while she bowed, her bonnet askew.

Unwittingly, Harriet Beecher Stowe had written the abolitionist's manifesto, although she did not consider herself an actual abolitionist who favored ending slavery everywhere, immediately, without adjustment or transition. She agreed with her father that abolitionists "were like men who would burn down their houses to get rid of the rats." She was not a crusader. She never considered herself an extremist, and she seldom took a strong position on any issue. She was a reformer, and there was an evangelical undercurrent to almost everything she wrote. Writing was her work, her way to make herself useful.

In the next thirty years, she wrote a book a year on average, plus innumerable essays, poems, children's stories, and magazine articles, many of which she published under the pseudonym Christopher Crowfield. Her novel, *The Minister's Wooing,* ran to fifty printings, and a magazine article, "The True Story of Lady Byron's Life," which appeared in the *Atlantic Monthly* in 1869, caused considerable furor.

During a second visit to England, Stowe had become friendly with Lord Byron's widow, who confided that Byron had committed incest with his half-sister, resulting in the birth of a child. Harriet kept the secret for thirteen years, well after Lady Byron's death. But when another of Byron's mistresses published her memoirs and portrayed Lady Byron as a self-righteous tyrant, Stowe decided to strike a blow on her friend's behalf and told the whole story.

Readers hurled all kinds of accusations at her, but she refused to respond. As with *Uncle Tom's Cabin*, Harriet wrote a book to justify her story about Byron. However, her standing with the American public was never the same.

Meanwhile, royalties poured in, but the more the Stowes had, the more they spent - on a huge Gothic villa in Hartford that was all gables and turrets, and was never finished completely; on a cotton plantation in Florida, where they planned to provide former slaves with a program of work and education; and later, when that failed, on an orange and lemon grove in Mandarin, Florida, "where the world is not," she said, and where she hoped her son Frederick might find his path in life.

Frederick had trouble with alcohol. His problem had started before the war, but at Gettysburg, he was hit in the head by a shell fragment and, his mother always believed, he was never himself again. "After that," one of her grandsons would write, "he not only was made drunk by the slightest amount of alcohol, but he could not resist taking it."

Calvin grew heavier and ever more distant, and lost interest in the everyday details of life. Harriet found fame increasingly difficult. As a celebrity, her correspondence requirements alone were draining.

In 1870, Frederick, unable to endure his mother's Florida experiment any longer, wrote her a touching apology and went to sea. He got as far as San Francisco, but then disappeared and was never heard from again. Harriet went to her grave with every confidence that he would return one day.

Harriet was hurt most grievously, though, by the Brooklyn Scandal. In November of 1872, a New York newspaper reported that her beloved brother Henry Ward Beecher, by then arguably the most popular preacher in America, had been conducting an affair with one of his married parishioners. For all the Beechers, the gossip was agonizing. A sensational trial resulted, the husband suing Beecher for alienation of his wife's affections. The trial dragged on for six months and was the talk of the country. Whether Beecher was guilty remains unproven. He denied everything, and the jury was unable to agree on a verdict, but as far as his sister was concerned, his character was never in question. She argued that the story was a slanderous fabrication, and she stood by him.

As time passed, Harriet bore her burdens with grace, seeming to become increasingly liberated from her past. She continued to pull back from her harsh Calvinist heritage, eventually rejecting it altogether. She had long since discarded the doctrine of original sin. Neither man nor nature was necessarily corrupt, she held. Hers was a faith of love and charity. Years before, her sister Catherine had been the first of the Beecher siblings to rebel against their father's traditional faith. When the Yale philosophy professor she was engaged to was lost at sea, Catherine had to confront the Calvinist conclusion that he was consigned to hell because he had never repented. She balked at that. In time, all of Lyman's children would leave the faith.

For Harriet, Calvinism was repugnant, a "glacial" doctrine, although she did admire the fervor it had given the Puritan colonists of her native New England. "They who had faced eternal ruin with an unflinching gaze," she wrote, "were not likely to shrink before the comparatively trivial losses and gains of any mere earthly conflict." Like many of her contemporaries, she lamented the decline of the Christian faith in America. Once from Florida she wrote: ". . . never did we have a more delicious spring. I never knew such altogether perfect weather. It is enough to make a saint out of the toughest old Calvinist that ever set his face as a flint. How do you think New England theology would have fared, if our fathers had landed here instead of on Plymouth Rock?"

Stowe became an Episcopalian, and she developed an open fondness for Europe (France and Italy especially), Rubens, elegant society, and Florida (". . . this wild, wonderful, bright, and vivid growth, that is all new, strange and unknown by name to me . . . "). She no longer viewed theater and dancing as sinful, rejecting the idea that "there was something radically corrupt and wicked in the body and in the physical system." She even had a small glass of claret on occasion.

Harriet was asked to go on "the lyceum," as the nineteenth-century lecture circuit was called. She needed the income, so at sixty-one, never having made a public speech before, she embarked on a new career. Although shy and inexperienced at first, she quickly gained confidence and became quite accomplished. "Her performance could hardly be called a reading," reported the Pittsburgh *Gazette*. "It was recitative and she seldom glanced at the book. Her voice betrayed the veritable Yankee twang. . . . Her voice is low, just tinged in the slightest with huskiness, but is quite musical. In manner, she was vivacious and gave life to many of the pages, more by suggestive action than by utterances. . . . She seemed perfectly possessed on the stage, and read with easy grace."

Stowe found she could move her audiences to great emotional heights, but also that she had a gift for making them laugh. She loved the life, despite the endless train rides, bad food, and dreary hotels. "I never sleep better than after a long day's ride," she wrote.

Despite the applause and adulation, Harriet changed little, either in attitude or appearance. Nothing seemed capable of changing her plain, earnest, often whimsical manner. She made a number of new friends that meant a great deal to her - Oliver Wendell Holmes and her neighbor Mark Twain were favorites. Henry Drummond, the Scottish writer, wrote, after a visit to Hartford: "Next door to Twain I found Mrs. Harriet Beecher Stowe, a wonderfully agile old lady, as fresh as a squirrel still, but with the face and air of a lion." And he concluded: "I have not been so taken with any one on this side of the Atlantic."

Harriet's affections for Calvin seemed to grow stronger. He became absorbed in Semitic studies, let his beard grow, and took to wearing a skullcap. Harriet began calling him My Old Rabbi. His apparitions took up more and more of his time, and for a while, he had nightly encounters with the devil, who came on horseback, Calvin said. Otherwise, his mind stayed quick and clear until the end, and she found him exceedingly good company.

In their last years, the Stowes had few financial worries. One book of Calvin's, *The Origin and History of the Books of the Bible*, sold well. Their affairs in general were capably managed by their twin daughters, Eliza and Harriet, maiden ladies who apparently had considerable "faculty."

Calvin died peacefully with Harriet at his bedside on August 6, 1886. She lived for another ten years, slipping gradually into senility.

To Oliver Wendell Holmes, she wrote: "I make no mental effort of any sort; my brain is tired out. It was a woman's brain and not a man's, and finally from sheer fatigue and exhaustion in the march and strife of life it gave out before the end was reached. And now I rest me, like a moored boat, rising and falling on the water, with loosened cordage and flapping sail." She was eighty-two.

During her final years, Stowe spent hours looking at picture books or went out gathering flowers. One writer described her as "a tiny withered figure in a garden hat." On occasion, she took long walks beside the river accompanied by her nurse. Sometimes, Twain would recall, she "would slip up behind a person who was deep in dreams and musings and fetch a war whoop that would jump that person out of his clothes."

Now and then, during moments of clarity, Harriet would talk about *Uncle Tom's Cabin*, the book that had just "come" to her in visions. Once, years earlier, when she was having trouble writing, she had said: "If there had been a grand preparatory blast of trumpets or had it been announced that Mrs. Stowe would do this or that, I think it likely I could not have written; but nobody expected anything . . . and so I wrote freely."

She died near midnight on July 1, 1896.

2
WAS IT
BUCHANAN'S WAR?
– ALLAN NEVINS

When James Buchanan took the oath of office as the fifteenth president of the United States on March 4, 1857, he seemed confident that the divisive issues facing the country could be settled. Instead, it was on his watch that the embers of the Civil War burst into open flame. Many historians believe that the decisions Buchanan made – and those he ducked – add up to one of the greatest failures of leadership in American history. And at least a few argue that a bolder president might have averted the war altogether.

The crisis played out in the raw territory of Kansas, where efforts to become a state were snarled in a bitter struggle between abolitionists, who wanted the new state to ban slavery, and Southern forces who insisted that it be a slave state. Buchanan declared that the will of the people should determine the issue of slavery, but he hoped to put off the choice for months or years – until "the number of actual residents in the Territory shall justify the formation of a constitution with a view to its admission as a State."

Two days after his inauguration, Buchanan took satisfaction in the Dred Scott decision handed down by Chief Justice Roger B. Taney, holding that Congress had no power to regulate slavery in the territories and that African-Americans, whether free or slaves, could not be citizens. That ruling voided the Missouri Compromise, which outlawed slavery north of the 36°30' line in the former Louisiana Territory. The Northern press denounced the decision, but the protests proved brief. Buchanan had seen his view sustained: Slavery now could enter any territory, and its white inhabitants could not keep it or drop it until they wrote their first constitution.

Since the creation of the territory in 1854, Kansas had been bitterly divided between proslavery and antislavery factions. Illinois Senator Stephen A. Douglas wrote the Kansas-Nebraska Act to open up thousands of new farms and support a Midwestern Transcontinental Railroad. But Douglas, a Democrat with presidential ambitions, wrote popular sovereignty into the act - largely so he would not have to take a side in the slavery debate. The clause meant that the people would vote to decide whether to allow slavery. It was intended to ease tensions, but it had the opposite effect. By 1857, Kansas was in chaos.

To sway elections, some 5,000 proslavery settlers – primarily from neighboring Missouri – went to Kansas in the spring of 1855. Horace Greeley, the abolitionist editor of the *New York Tribune,* called them "border ruffians." They intimidated voters into installing a proslavery legislature. In response, Free-Soil settlers, also known as "Jayhawkers," flooded into Kansas. A Free-Soil convention in Topeka refused to recognize the proslavery legislature and adopted a constitution that slavery supporters rejected. The fight quickly escalated.

Greeley coined the term Bleeding Kansas to describe both the political pandemonium and the physical violence that ensued. While a war of words was waged in Congress and lecture halls, people on both sides assembled small armies.

Abolitionist John Brown led a force into Kansas in October 1855, and the next month, clashed with 1,500 Missourians. The fighting had been sparked by the killing of Charles Dow, a Free-Soil man, by a proslavery settler in Lawrence, Kansas. The so-called "Wakarusa War" left only one other man dead – Thomas Barber, a wool-maker from Indiana, who had been drawn into the Free-State movement. The following spring, Lawrence was again the scene of violence, as proslavery Missourians invaded, burned the Free State Hotel, destroyed two newspaper offices, and ransacked homes and stores. Days later, Brown and his army raided a proslavery settlement north of Pottawatomie Creek, pulled five men from their homes, and hacked them to death with broadswords. That touched off a series of retaliatory raids by both sides, and the conflict escalated.

That same month, Republican Massachusetts Senator Charles Sumner delivered his "Crime Against Kansas" speech, denouncing slavery. In it, he ridiculed sixty-year-old South Carolina Senator Andrew Butler, who had co-authored the Kansas-Nebraska Act with Douglas, for his proslavery position. South Carolina Congressman Preston Brooks, Butler's cousin, was outraged, and two days later, nearly beat Sumner to death with his cane in the Senate chamber. The episode made Sumner a martyr in the North and Brooks a hero in the South, further inflaming passions.

Still, Buchanan believed the people of Kansas held the power to determine the territory's fate. In theory, the president could dispatch a new, impartial governor. And if the people wanted statehood, they could vote for a new constitutional convention. Then the voters could give the nation its sixteenth slave state or its seventeenth free state.

In reality, the idea that the people of Kansas would respond with dispassionate reason was unlikely. Behind the two Kansas parties were equally determined Northerners and Southerners. "Slavery will now yield a greater profit in Kansas," wrote a propagandist in the Southern magazine De Bow's Review, "either to hire out or cultivate the soil, than any other place." Meanwhile, Yankees were subsidizing their own settlers, who had been at a disadvantage competing with wealthy slave owners. "I know people," said poet and abolitionist Ralph Waldo Emerson, "who are making haste to reduce their expenses and pay their debts . . . to save and earn for the benefit of Kansas emigrants."

The stage was set for a brief, fateful drama. It would feature Buchanan and Douglas, shape Abraham Lincoln's national reputation, and determine whether the North and South would remain united. That drama was called Lecompton. And Douglas went to his grave believing that the Civil War would have been avoided if Buchanan had behaved differently.

Sixty-six-year-old James Buchanan had not entered eagerly into the role of president, although his career had been distinguished enough. Born in a log cabin in Cove Gap, Pennsylvania, he studied law, served as an army private in the War of 1812, and was elected to the Pennsylvania House of

Representatives. He served five terms in Congress before President Andrew Jackson appointed him minister to Russia in 1832. Between 1834 and 1845, he held a U.S. Senate seat, and during James Polk's presidency, he served as secretary of state. While his name was being bandied about by Democrats seeking a nominee for the presidential election of 1856, Buchanan was in England, where he was minister to the Court of St. James. He told Nathaniel Hawthorne, who in January 1855 was serving as American consul in Liverpool, "as regards his prospects for the Presidency . . . that his mind was fully made up, and that he would never be a candidate, and that he had expressed this decision to his friends in such a way as to put it out of his own power to change it . . . that it was now too late, and that he was too old."

Still, Buchanan did not discourage the movement on his behalf. He never declared his candidacy, but let his popularity speak for itself at the nominating convention. "The people have taken the next presidency out of the hands of the politicians," Jonathan Foltz, a friend from Pennsylvania, told Buchanan, ". . . the people and not your political friends will place you there," and they had.

For all his credentials, however, Buchanan's non-candidacy was tell-tale: His primary characteristic was irresolution. "Even among close friends," noted one Southern senator, "he very rarely expressed his opinions at all upon disputed questions, except in language especially marked with a cautious circumspection almost amounting to timidity." Industrious, capable, tactful, and well-read, Buchanan was also humorless, calculating, and pliable. Above all, his contemporaries said, he had no strong convictions. Polk had described his secretary of state as an old woman and said, "It is one of his weaknesses that he takes on and magnifies small matters into great and undeserved importance."

Buchanan could be stubborn and lash out at friends and enemies alike. As the crisis over the territories deepened, he hoped to move through it and leave office with the Union intact, leaving his successor to avert or weather the storm.

The Supreme Court's Dred Scott ruling had been less sweeping than Buchanan had hoped. In his inaugural address, he had proclaimed that the ruling would "speedily and finally" resolve the question of slavery, and he would "cheerfully submit, whatever this may be." He had greatly underestimated the powers at play. They were divided into three main groups - the proslavery group, which included David Atchison of Missouri, Jefferson Davis of Mississippi, Alexander Stephens of Georgia, Robert Toombs of Georgia, and John Slidell of Louisiana; the free-soil group, led by Salmon Chase of Ohio and William Seward of New York; and the popular sovereignty group, led by Douglas.

Unlike Buchanan, all three groups were fierce in their convictions. One side saw slavery as a social and economic good and demanded not only the right to expand slavery into the territories but also federal protection against any local action to stop it. The abolitionists, who soon found a voice in Abraham Lincoln, held that slavery had been condemned by the Founding Fathers, was increasingly outlawed by the civilized world, and should be excluded from all territories, present or future. Douglas, with his sovereignty backers, did not believe slavery was a moral issue. He did not care whether slavery was voted up or down, only that the vote was fair.

While Buchanan hoped to pass the issue on to the next administration, Lincoln pursued the fight. Once the country accepted non-expansion of slavery, Lincoln argued, it would accept the idea of extinction. Once this crisis was met and passed, Americans would decide when and how slavery might be ended.

Buchanan associated with proslavery Southerners but did not hold to their beliefs. He was most closely aligned with Douglas's sovereignty group, which took the Dred Scott doctrine a step further. Local legislation and action, Douglas said, could exclude slavery even before a territory became a state, and federal action was uncalled for.

Kansas's proslavery leaders had powerful allies in Washington - Southerners such as Treasury Secretary Howell Cobb, House Speaker James Orr, Senator Slidell, and Secretary of the Interior Jacob Thompson. Having gained control of the territory, they intended to keep it, and soon, Buchanan would buckle under their pressure, putting him at odds with Douglas.

The proslavery Kansas legislature – grossly misrepresentative of the majority of its settlers, who opposed slavery – was organizing a convention to write a new state constitution. In the capital of Lecompton, a handful of Southern supporters, led by a few political fanatics, would have the power to determine the future of the nation.

The new Kansas constitution was meant to cancel out the document produced by the Free-Soil party in Topeka. To ensure its proslavery stance, a bill was forced through that allowed the legislators to control the election of delegates to the convention. It called for sheriffs and their deputies to register white residents in March 1857, for probate judges to approve the sheriffs' lists of qualified voters, and for county commissioners to choose election judges. The county commissioners had themselves not been elected but were chosen – and thus controlled - by the legislature.

When Governor John W. Geary, a Democrat appointed by President Franklin Pierce, vetoed the bill, the legislature immediately re-passed it. And when threats against his life increased until people began to lay bets that he would be assassinated within forty days, Geary resigned and traveled east to warn the country of imminent danger.

On his way to Washington, Geary alerted the press that a convention was about to drag Kansas before Congress with a proslavery constitution. This convention would have a free hand, he pointed out, because the bill just passed made no provision for a popular vote. One legislator admitted that the plan was to avoid popular submission; he proposed inserting a clause to guard against the possibility that Congress might return the constitution for a referendum. The *Missouri Democrat* editorialized, "The felon legislature has provided as effectually for getting the desired result as Louis Napoleon did for getting himself elected Emperor." This was an ironic commentary on Douglas's maxim: "Let the voice of the people rule."

But Douglas saw his principles and political future at stake. When his Kansas-Nebraska Act was passed, he had promised the North that a free, full, and fair election would decide the future of the two territories. He had notified the South that Kansas was almost certain to be free soil. Now he confidently asserted that Buchanan would never permit a breach of fair procedure. He worked with the president to persuade former Secretary of the Treasury Robert J. Walker to go to Kansas in Geary's place as the new governor. Douglas knew that if he consented to a betrayal of popular sovereignty, he would be ruined politically in his home state of Illinois.

For a brief moment in the spring of 1857, Buchanan seemed to stand firm. He instructed Walker to put the new constitution before the people, stating that "they must be protected in the exercise of their right of voting for or against that instrument, and the fair expression of the popular will must not be interrupted by fraud or violence."

It is not surprising that the proslavery advocates in Kansas forced their plans despite all Buchanan's rhetoric and Walker's efforts to uphold him. With four-fifths of the people already against them and the odds growing greater every year, they knew their only way to win was through brazen trickery. They were aware that the South, which believed that a fair division would give Kansas to slavery and Nebraska to freedom, expected them to stand firm.

The abolitionist *Kansas News* described the constitutional convention in Lecompton, in which forty-eight of the sixty delegates came from slave states, as "broken-down political hacks, demagogues, fire-eaters, perjurers, ruffians, ballot-box stuffers, and loafers." But before the convention concluded with the shout, "Now, boys, let's come and take a drink!" it had written a constitution.

That document went against everything Buchanan and Douglas believed. Although it contained numerous controversial provisions, such as limiting banking to one institution and barring free blacks, the main document was not submitted to a general vote. Voters in the referendum could cast their ballots for the "constitution with slavery" or the "constitution with no slavery." But "no slavery" meant only that no additional slaves would be imported while the 200 slaves already in Kansas would remain, with a constitutional guarantee that they would not be freed. And whenever the state's proslavery faction could get control of the legislature, it could open the door for more slaves. The referendum was boycotted by free-soilers, and even so the result was tainted; half of the 6,000 favorable ballots were said to be fraudulent. But the Lecompton constitution, together with a competing document from the antislavery faction, was sent to Congress for ratification.

The South, grossly misinformed about events in Kansas, believed it was being cheated. The Northern free-soilers had vowed that no new slave state would ever be admitted into the Union. Angry Southerners thought the Yankees had unscrupulously used their wealth and numbers to influence decisions in Kansas.

Jefferson Davis declared: "You have made it a political war. We are on the defensive. How far are you to push us?" Threats of secession mingled with Southern denunciations. "Sir," Senator Alfred Iverson of Georgia said, "I believe that the time will come when . . . slave States will be compelled, in vindication of their rights, interests, and honor, to separate from . . . free states, and erect an independent confederacy, and I am not sure, sir, that the time is not at hand."

Southern Cabinet members Cobb, Thompson, and John B. Floyd had taken the measure of Buchanan's pusillanimity. They worked to control the tremulous president by playing on Buchanan's hatred of Republicans and his dislike of Douglas.

Henry S. Foote, a former senator from Mississippi and an enemy of Jefferson Davis, saw Lecompton for what it was and hurried to Washington. "It was unfortunately of no avail that these efforts to reassure Mr. Buchanan were at that time essayed by myself and others," Foote wrote. "He had already become thoroughly panic-stricken; the howling of the bulldog of secession had fairly frightened him out of his wits, and he ingloriously resolved to yield without further resistance to the decrial and vilification to which he had been so acrimoniously subjected."

The Washington correspondent of the New Orleans *Picayune* later described how Buchanan was intimidated: "The President was informed in November, 1857, that the States of Alabama, Mississippi, and South Carolina, and perhaps others, would hold conventions and secede from the Union if the Lecompton Constitution, which established slavery, should not be accepted by Congress. The reason was that these States, supposing that the South had been cheated out of Kansas, were, whether right or wrong, determined to revolt. The President believed this. Senator Hunter, of Virginia, to my knowledge, believed it. Many other eminent men did, and perhaps not without reason."

Buchanan, with no more imagination than nerve, began to yield to this Southern storm. By November 1857, he had surrendered. When Congress met in December, he upheld the Lecompton Constitution. Seldom in American history has a chief executive made a greater error or missed a larger opportunity. Franklin Pierce wrote: "I had considerable hopes of Mr. Buchanan - I really thought he was a statesman - but I have now come to the settled conclusion that he is just the damndest old fool that has ever occupied the presidential chair. He has deliberately walked overboard with his eyes open - let him drown, for he must."

As Buchanan shrank from influence, Douglas entered the fray. Political necessity demanded his action: Illinois would not have sent him back to the

Senate the following year if he had not fought to defeat Lecompton in Congress. But it was also a matter of principle for Douglas.

"By God, Sir!" he exclaimed, "I made James Buchanan, and by God, sir, I will unmake him!" Friends told him that the Southern Democrats would destroy his career and reputation. "I have taken a through ticket," Douglas replied, "and checked my baggage." He quickly confronted Buchanan in the White House and denounced the Lecompton policy. When the president reminded him how Jackson had crushed two party rebels, Douglas snorted, "Mr. President, I wish you to remember that General Jackson is dead."

For the Southern extremists who had coerced Buchanan, Douglas's scorn was unbounded. He told the Washington correspondent of the *Chicago Journal* that he had begun his battle against a single bad measure, but his argument against Lecompton had brought the whole "slave power" down on him like a pack of wolves. He added: "In making the fight against this power, I was enabled to stand off and view the men with whom I had been acting; I was ashamed I had ever been caught in such company; they are a set of unprincipled demagogues, bent upon perpetuating slavery, and by the exercise of that unequal and unfair power, to control the government or break up the Union; and I intend to prevent their doing either."

Led by Douglas, Northern Democrats joined abolitionist Republicans to oppose Lecompton. Allies in Kansas uncovered the fraudulent ballots in the referendum, and a new vote was proposed; at the same time, two more constitutions were drafted, both of them banning slavery. On April 1, 1858, Lecompton was defeated in the House of Representatives.

When the vote was announced, a wild cheer rolled through the galleries. Francis P. Blair, Jackson's friend, carried the news to the dying Missouri Senator Thomas Hart Benton. Benton could barely speak, but his exultation was unbounded. "In energetic whispers," Blair wrote, "he told his visitor that the same men who had sought to destroy the republic in 1850 were at the bottom of this accursed Lecompton business. Among the greatest of his consolations in dying was the consciousness that the House of Representatives had baffled these treasonable schemes and put the heels of the people on the necks of the traitors."

The administration covered its retreat by offering Kansans the hastily concocted English Bill, under which Kansas would enter the Union as a free state. The Kansas plotters had been bested. But Southern secessionists had gained fresh strength and greater boldness from their success in coercing Buchanan's administration.

The Lecompton struggle left an interesting set of

aftereffects. It elevated Douglas to a new plane; he had been a Democratic strategist, but after this he became a national leader. It sharpened the issues which that summer and fall were to frame the Lincoln-Douglas debates in Illinois. At the same time, it exacerbated the schism between Southern Democrats and northwestern Democrats and helped pave the way to that disruption of the party which preceded the disruption of the nation. In Kansas, it planted new seeds of dissension, which resulted in fresh conflicts between free-soilers and Missouri invaders and led to some of the darkest days of the Civil War. The Lecompton battle discredited Buchanan in the eyes of most Northerners, strengthened Southern conviction of his weakness, and left his administration materially and morally weaker.

Foote wrote later that he knew that a scheme for destroying the Union "had long been on foot in the South" and that its leaders "were only waiting for the enfeebling of the Democratic Party in the North, and the general triumph of Free-soilism as a consequence thereof, to alarm the whole South into acquiescence in their policy." Buchanan's support of the Lecompton constitution gave the plotters a position of strength.

Douglas took the same view. He knew, thanks to inside information in 1857, he later told the Senate, that four states were threatening Buchanan with secession. Had their bluff been called, the leaders of the movement would, he believed, have been discredited, and their conspiracy would have collapsed. They would have been so routed that the Democratic Party schism in 1860 might never have taken place, and if it had, secession in 1861 would have been impossible.

3

GOD'S CHOSEN INSTRUMENT

– STEPHEN W. SEARS

General George B. McClellan had a gift for the dramatic gesture, and on the afternoon of September 14, 1862, at South Mountain in western Maryland, he surpassed himself.

Before him on the smoke-wreathed mountaintop, his army was locked in combat with the Confederates. Nearby artillery batteries added their thunder to the rattle of musketry, and columns of reinforcements in Union blue were winding their way up the mountainside. McClellan sat motionless on his horse with his arm extended, pointing his passing troops toward the fighting. They cheered him until they were hoarse, one of them recalled, and some broke ranks to swarm around the martial figure and indulge in the "most extravagant demonstrations."

The tableau, however, was not all that it seemed. "God has seldom given an army a greater victory than this," McClellan announced when it was over, but, in fact, the outcome of South Mountain was far less decisive than he believed. Everything about it was perfectly characteristic of George McClellan.

Known affectionately among his men as "Little Mac," McClellan was short and slight, but made up for it with his erect posture, superb horsemanship and impeccably tailored uniform, with the three stars of a major general polished to a high sheen. He had a talent for generating illusions; people found it easy to see in him what they wanted to see. His admirers viewed him as the unstained hero who would crush the rebellion and restore the Union. To his detractors, he was the failed hero, responsible for snatching defeat from the jaws of victory and prolonging a war that was growing more terrible each day.

McClellan seemed to be a strong, decisive commander, a general with an unmatched gift for organizing and motivating his troops. But in battle, he was all but paralyzed by a loss of will and a fear of defeat. He was portrayed as the innocent victim of political partisanship, when in fact he deliberately involved himself in the political issues of the war. He was accused of being secretly in sympathy with the South and secession, yet no one believed more strongly in perpetual Union than McClellan. In 1864, he ran for president on a peace platform and was backed by 45 percent of the voters in his opposition to Abraham Lincoln's wartime leadership. McClellan saw a special significance in this outcome. Certain that he had been chosen by God to lead the Union in war, he explained his electoral defeat as "a part of the grand plan of the Almighty, who designed that the cup should be drained even to the bitter dregs, that the people might be made worthy of being saved."

History is widely divided on his impact, with little to no neutral ground. "McClellan still possesses a rare power to inspire either admiration or contempt," Richard N. Current wrote in 1958. McClellan biographies bear such subtitles as "Shield of the Union" and "The Man Who Saved the Union," yet in a study of Northern commanders, Kenneth P. Williams dismissed him as "merely an attractive but vain and unstable man, with considerable military knowledge, who sat a horse well and wanted to be President." Two distinguished historians of the Civil War era, James G. Randall and Allan Nevins, judged him very differently. "Nothing worth while in the East was done on the Northern side in 1862 except under McClellan," Randall wrote. But Nevins considered him psychologically unfit for his role, timid and overcautious and lacking the "central quality of a great commander," the will to fight. McClellan excelled only in not taking risks,

Nevins concluded; "this spirit would save the army and lose the nation."

McClellan's commander-in-chief, President Abraham Lincoln, bore patiently for months with the general's grandiose pride, condescending attitude, and ignoring of orders. Lincoln kept hoping that McClellan would finally live up to his billing and pressed him again and again to make use of the vast army he had trained. The president lost patience only when McClellan squandered a chance to capture the rebel capital, Richmond, and suffered a string of defeats at the hands of General Robert E. Lee in the Battles of Seven Days.

The first and perhaps ablest of McClellan's defenders was McClellan himself. His *Report* on his wartime service, published in 1864, was filled with letters, dispatches, and other documents making the case "that he is a great military genius, after all," according to James Russell Lowell. A posthumously published memoir, *McClellan's Own Story*, and the general's private papers offer more insight into this contradictory figure.

George McClellan was highly dogmatic, with fixed notions about the object of the war and how it should be fought, as well as a distorted mental image of the enemy. He tolerated no departure from these views, nor any dissent about them. He was "God's chosen instrument" to save the Union, his path was the chosen path, and those who raised objections - whether president or general - were at best ignorant and at worst traitors. This stubborn rigidity earned him many enemies among his allies.

His war service spanned about eighteen months and was marked by volatile swings from glorious success to miserable failure. In mid-1861, campaigning in western Virginia, he gained notice as the North's first military hero – if only because the Union had suffered a long string of embarrassing and depressing defeats. After minor victories at Philippi and Rich Mountain, in which the Confederates retreated after offering little resistance, McClellan was dubbed "the Napoleon of the Present War" by the *New York Herald*.

Promoted rapidly to high command - including, for four months, command of all Union armies - he was credited with organizing the Army of the Potomac, only to lose much of his luster for his chronic reluctance to commit that army to battle. His Peninsula Campaign against Richmond in the spring of 1862, the largest military operation of the war, was on the brink of capturing the Confederate capital before it ended in repulse and defeat.

McClellan was deposed as General-in-Chief but remained in charge of the Army of the Potomac while General John Pope and his new Army of Virginia were ordered to march on Richmond again. But when Pope lost the Second Battle of Bull Run, McClellan was recalled to combine both armies, restore morale, and beat back Lee's invasion of Maryland.

That set up the Battle of South Mountain on September 14, 1862. Positioning for a drive north across the Potomac, Lee had riskily divided his army, and a copy of his orders had fallen into McClellan's hands. By pushing through three gaps in the South Mountain ridge that divided eastern Maryland from the western part of the state, McClellan had a chance to rout half of Lee's forces. Lee hastily reinforced the three passes, but McClellan easily took one of them and ended the day's battle on the verge of capturing the other two. Tellingly, he never committed the reserve forces that might have tipped the balance. Lee retreated, but McClellan failed to pursue the beaten troops; that gave Lee time to reunite his army, and set up the bloody Battle of Antietam three days later.

At Antietam, McClellan won another partial victory, missing the key opportunity to destroy the Confederate army and set the North on the road to winning the war. Seven weeks later, in November 1862, he was again relieved of command, and his military career was over. McClellan's greatest delusion was that none of what happened was his fault. At first he blamed his failures on General-in-Chief Winfield Scott. Then, after he managed to get Scott's title, he blamed War Secretary Edwin Stanton and Lincoln himself.

His early career was meteoric. McClellan started his military training a year earlier than most, enrolling in the United States Military Academy at the age of fifteen. He graduated in 1846, second in his class of fifty-nine cadets. As an engineering officer in the Mexican War, he was promoted to lieutenant and then to captain, earning a reputation as a brilliant strategist with a deep understanding of military history and theory.

In the mid-1850s, he was the protégé of Secretary of War (and future Confederate president) Jefferson Davis, who sent him to Europe to observe the war in the Crimea and to evaluate the armies of the major powers. To this experience, McClellan added four years of civilian employment as a railroad executive - useful training for managing military logistics. As an army friend said of him, he was well known to be "chock full of big war science."

After the Confederate bombardment of Fort Sumter touched off the Civil War on April 12, 1861, McClellan was the most sought-after former army officer in the North. He was offered command of troops in Ohio, Pennsylvania, and New York. On April 23, ten days after Sumter's surrender, he was named major general of volunteers and commander of Ohio's army; ten days after that, he was heading the Department of the Ohio and the main Union forces west of the Alleghenies.

Commissioned major general, he ranked second only to the aging General Scott.

Visiting Washington, McClellan was lionized – and relished every moment of it. "I find myself in a new & strange position here," he wrote to his wife, Nelly. "Presdt, Cabinet, Genl Winfield Scott & all deferring to me – by some strange operation of magic I seem to have become the power of the land. I almost think that were I to win some small success now I could become Dictator or anything else that might please me – but nothing of that kind would please me – I won't be Dictator. Admirable self denial!"

At his headquarters in Cincinnati, McClellan energetically organized and drilled the thousands of volunteers who had rushed to the defense of the Union. Four days after assuming command, he sent to Washington a plan for defeating the rebellion and bringing "the war to a speedy close," the first such scheme by a Northern general. Lincoln received it politely, but largely ignored it.

When Virginia sent troops west, McClellan countered with an expeditionary force. Without consulting Washington, he issued a proclamation assuring Virginians there would be no interference with their slaves. "Not only will we abstain from all such interference," he promised, "but we will on the contrary with an iron hand, crush any attempt at insurrection on their part." He quickly apologized for the indiscretion. If he had misjudged the case, he wrote Lincoln, "a terrible mistake has been made, for the proclamation is regarded as expressing the views of the Presdt, & I have not intimated that it was prepared without authority." His promise was not, in fact, contrary to the government's policy at the time. Its real significance was that McClellan had badly overstepped his authority and publicly committed the Union army to the protection of Southern slavery. The incident also gave substance to later accusations that he was a Southern sympathizer.

After less than a month and his two minor victories at Philippi Races and Rich Mountain, McClellan's 11,000-man army proclaimed triumph in western Virginia. The general telegraphed Washington, "Our success is complete & secession is killed in this country." In 1863, the region would join the Union as the new state of West Virginia.

The timing of McClellan's victories was fortunate. A week after he sent his telegram, the Union army was defeated disastrously at the First Battle of Bull Run. On July 22, 1861, thirty-four-year-old George McClellan was summoned to the capital to take command of what he christened the Army of the Potomac. He had demonstrated skill in military administration, but chief among his qualifications, he had won a battle, and just then that was unique.

Two weeks later, McClellan raised the alarm that Washington was in "imminent danger" of assault by

100,000 rebels. This count was entirely McClellan's invention, and it set the precedent for all those that followed. When Winfield Scott rejected his extraordinary arithmetic and insisted that the capital was in no danger, McClellan declared war on him. "I do not know whether he is a *dotard* or a *traitor!*" McClellan said, ". . . he is a perfect imbecile." Under pressure from McClellan and his allies, President Lincoln accepted Scott's removal. On November 1, 1861, McClellan took his place as head of all the armies.

In the months to come, McClellan always assumed his army was outnumbered by Confederates. During the first days of the Peninsula Campaign in 1862, he reported he was facing 100,000 enemy troops at Yorktown - a figure that grew to 200,000 by the time he reached the outskirts of Richmond three months later. When Lee struck out northward against Pope, McClellan gave the Rebels 120,000 men; he stuck to that estimation throughout the Maryland campaign.

Of course, the opposite was true: In every battle, the Union army had the advantage of size - at Antietam, by almost two to one. Some of the blame for McClellan's confusion can be attributed to incompetent collectors of intelligence, notably the future private detective Allan Pinkerton and Alfred Pleasonton, his cavalry chief. But these men supplied McClellan only with what he expected: confirmation of his own convictions. There is nothing to suggest McClellan deliberately fabricated these figures to gain reinforcements or to excuse defeat. Letters to his wife suggest he was totally convinced.

McClellan also imagined Southern soldiers to be better trained, faster, and blessed with higher morale than his own men, and he expressed great respect for Southern generals. The one Confederate general McClellan disparaged was Robert E. Lee; ironically, he told Lincoln that he considered Lee "too cautious & weak under grave responsibility . . . likely to be timid & irresolute in action." But the Confederate army as a whole was, in McClellan's mind, capable of tremendous feats; he saw any possible maneuver, no matter how improbable, as fact.

As general-in-chief, McClellan geared all operations to the support of the Army of the Potomac, which he believed would advance like a juggernaut to crush the rebellion in one Napoleonic stroke. Even his conviction that he was outnumbered did not deter him from this idea of a single grand campaign. He viewed secession as a political aberration; once defeated in a major test of arms, he believed, the Confederacy's leaders would come to the peace table willing to discuss reunion. If, in the process, Southern civilians and their property (including their slaves) were carefully protected, the Union might be restored without social upheaval.

McClellan was a conservative Democrat and believed strongly that abolishing slavery and confiscating property would only embitter the South and force the Rebels to fight to the last ditch. He viewed with infinite dread, he wrote in 1862, "any policy which tends to render impossible the reconstruction of the Union and to make this contest simply a useless effusion of blood." Unconditional surrender must not be a war objective.

He expected the issue of slavery to be resolved in due course by gradual, compensated emancipation, guarding the rights of both slaves and masters. "When the day of adjustment comes," he told his wife, "I will . . . throw my sword into the scale to force an improvement in the condition of those poor blacks." But first the issue of war must be resolved. Soon after arriving in Washington, he met with prominent abolitionists, including Massachusetts Senator Charles Sumner, to make it clear "that I was fighting for my country & the Union, not for abolition and the Republican party."

In this same spirit, he wrote to President Lincoln on July 8, 1862, urging that radical Republican schemes such as the confiscation of property, reorganization of territory, and forcible abolition of slavery should not be "contemplated for a moment." The document, sent from his camp near Harrison's Landing in Virginia as McClellan was preparing to abandon his Peninsula Campaign, was not intended only for the president. He urged its circulation within the administration as the "policy which ought to govern this contest on our part." Lincoln did not respond, leaving McClellan little hope of steering the government away from the "radical & inhumane views to which it seemed inclined." In 1864, McClellan made the Harrison's Landing letter his platform for the presidency.

McClellan always described the Army of the Potomac as "my" army; it "is my army as much as any army ever belonged to the man that created it," he insisted. By the end of 1861, there were 192,000 men in his army, and McClellan sought to secure their loyalty by becoming as familiar to them as their company officers. He staged grand reviews and inspected the camps almost daily. On campaign, he constantly rode the lines to show himself to the troops, who cheered their "Little Mac." To comparisons with Napoleon, he said proudly, "I don't believe that Napoleon even ever possessed the love & confidence of his men more fully than I do of mine."

These displays of loyalty were not entirely spontaneous. On the march, he was preceded by an officer shouting, "McClellan's coming, boys! McClellan's coming! Three cheers for McClellan!" Still, the affection was both genuine and mutual. "You have no idea how the men brighten up now, when I go among them - I can see every eye glisten," he told his wife. "Yesterday they nearly pulled me to pieces in one [regiment]. You never heard such yelling." Addressing his troops on the eve of the Peninsula Campaign, he urged that they "ever bear in mind that my fate is linked with yours. . . . I am to watch over you as a parent over his children; and you know that your General loves you from the depths of his heart." Looking back on these early months of the war, a regimental chaplain wrote, "The truth is, our magnificent army much needed a transcendent leader, and the crisis prompted us both to crave and expect one fit for the occasion - one whom we could afford to idolize."

Yet the idol, as the chaplain later bitterly acknowledged, proved to have feet of clay. By the summer of 1862, McClellan's failure to press the attack had provided time for Lee to organize a defense. McClellan's army had been driven from the gates of Richmond in the Seven Days' Battles by Lee's relentless attacks, and his grand campaign lay in ruins. To explain to his army what had happened, McClellan conjured up a triumph over adversity, if not a victory. They had not retreated, he insisted, but only executed a change of base "by a flank movement, always regarded as the most hazardous of military expedients." He invented "vastly superior" enemy forces, against which, "without hope of reinforcements," they had bravely survived the week of bloody fighting. "Your conduct ranks you among the celebrated armies of history," he told his men.

In further support of this delusion, McClellan shifted all blame to the government. He claimed the administration had deliberately withheld reinforcements to ensure his defeat at Richmond - to forestall a peace settlement on McClellan's terms. Republican radicals, he claimed, would never permit the war to end until abolitionism had triumphed. By this "abominable design," he asserted, his enemies in Washington had "done their best to sacrifice as noble an Army as ever marched to battle." As he intended, his charges soon reached the newspapers, which gave them weight – and exasperated the president.

But the abominable design existed only in McClellan's mind. On the eve of the Seven Days' Battles, he had more troops available to him than his plans had ever called for. He did not lack men, only a will to fight. At the beginning of the Confederate offensive, he had telegraphed his wife, "I believe we will surely win & that the enemy is falling into a trap. I shall allow the enemy to cut off our communications in order to ensure success." Clearly, he recognized the opportunity for a counterstrike presented by Lee's bold but risky flanking attack, but when it was time to act, he became unnerved and ordered a retreat. In the ensuing Battles of the Seven Days, McClellan posted himself far from the field and let his commanders fight without direction. His army survived not because of him, but despite him.

Nevertheless, he convinced himself that Lincoln and Stanton were to blame for not sending him more troops and supplies. He sent Stanton a telegram so insolent that the telegraph operator in Washington deleted the most provocative parts before delivering it. The wire said, among other things, "If I save this army now, I tell you plainly I owe no thanks to any other persons in Washington. You have done your best to sacrifice this army." For Lincoln, it was the last straw. McClellan lost his post as commanding general, and Pope took over the assault on Richmond.

While a majority of McClellan's men accepted his explanation for the Peninsula failure, there was a strong undercurrent of disillusion. Francis C. Barlow, a regimental commander involved in the bitterest fighting during the Seven Days, wrote home that many officers and men "are disgusted with & have lost confidence in McClellan & are disgusted with attempts of the papers to make him out a victorious hero. . . . The stories of his being everywhere among the men in the fights are all untrue." Others shared the puzzlement of the soldier who wrote from Harrison's Landing, "Either we have made an inglorious *skedaddle* or a brilliant retreat." In the press, in Congress, and in the army, the debate over McClellan's generalship grew heated.

In the Second Battle of Bull Run that August of 1862,

McClellan was accused of deliberately withholding reinforcements from General Pope to ensure his defeat. He wrote his wife that he considered Pope a "villain" who was certain "to bring defeat upon any cause that employs him." Thus, McClellan had held back two army corps under his command; the only aid they gave Pope was to cover his retreat. Pope might have lost the battle anyway, but having those 25,000 reinforcements twenty-four hours earlier certainly would have improved his chances.

On September 2, 1862, in one of the critical decisions of his presidency and against the strong opposition of his cabinet, Lincoln fired Pope and handed the command back to McClellan. The president argued that the army was suffering from a crisis of confidence, for which there was only one remedy. "McClellan has the army with him," Lincoln said. To his secretary, John Hay, the President explained, "We must use what tools we have. There is no man in the Army who can man these fortifications and lick these troops of ours into shape half as well as he. If he can't fight himself, he excels in making others ready to fight." McClellan wrote his wife, "I only consent to take it for my country's sake & with the humble hope that God has called me to it." Five days later, he set out to challenge the Confederate invasion of Maryland.

McClellan gauged the Maryland campaign as the high point of his military career. "I feel some little pride," he told his wife, "in having with a beaten and demoralized army defeated Lee so utterly, & saved the North so completely." On the day after the climactic struggle at Antietam, he wrote her, "Those in whose judgment I rely tell me that I fought the battle splendidly & that it was a masterpiece of art." Every year for the rest of his life, he celebrated September 17, the anniversary of the battle.

The boast that Maryland and Pennsylvania were now safe revealed the extent of McClellan's delusion. "The hearts of 10 million people sunk within them when McClellan raised that shout," Lincoln remarked.

The general's failures in Maryland were manifest. At South Mountain, he had settled for a minor victory instead of seizing the chance to destroy half of Lee's scattered forces. At Antietam three days later, his outmanned opponent was vulnerable to a degree not matched again until the last doomed hours at Appomattox. Ezra A. Carman, a Northern veteran of Antietam and author of the definitive tactical study of the battle, wrote that on that day, "More errors were committed by the Union commander than in any other battle of the war." The real consequence of the battle was not the survival of the Army of the Potomac, but the escape of the Army of Northern Virginia.

After the war, in a sympathetic evaluation of General McClellan, Ulysses S. Grant suggested he had been undone by his too-rapid rise to high command. Had he instead "fought his way along and up," as Grant himself had done, perhaps in the end McClellan would have won "as high distinction as any." But most historians judge that McClellan lacked the capacity to grow as a commander; he was as good a general on his first campaigns as he ever became. On every battlefield from western Virginia to Maryland, he demonstrated the same fundamental fault in his military character: He could never force himself to press relentlessly for victory, to commit his reserves when they would do the most good, and to accept the losses necessary for winning.

McClellan himself confirmed this judgment. "I am tired of the sickening sight of the battlefield, with its mangled corpses & poor suffering wounded!" he wrote his wife during the Peninsula Campaign. "Victory has no charms for me when purchased at such cost."

Lincoln had sensed this flaw in his general even before the fighting on the Peninsula; he had seen in McClellan precisely the defects of timidity and lack of resolve that McClellan had projected onto Lee. As the president told a friend then, McClellan "had the capacity to make arrangements properly for a great conflict, but as the hour for action approached he became nervous and oppressed with the responsibility and hesitated to meet the crisis."

The president detected no real change in McClellan even after his claim of victory at Antietam. Despite having defeated Lee "so utterly," the general was soon crediting his opponent with 150,000 men – twice as many as he actually had – and with being just as dangerous as ever. Through the fall of 1862, McClellan raised every objection to renewing the contest until Lincoln, his patience exhausted, again relieved him of command. In reporting the news to his wife, McClellan cloaked his record in one final illusion: "we have tried to do what was right - if we have failed it was not our fault."

McClellan's military legacy was crippling. The Potomac army was left with an army-sized inferiority complex - a belief that the best it could hope for was survival against great adversity and overwhelming numbers.

McClellan's deliberate efforts to link the army's morale with the popularity of its general had consequences that were equally unfortunate. Lincoln picked his successor, Ambrose Burnside, not so much for his military abilities as for the fact that he was well liked by the men. Lincoln hoped the troops would follow Burnside as faithfully as they had McClellan. Hardly a month later, however, Burnside suffered a crushing defeat at Fredericksburg, and the army's morale collapsed along with Burnside's reputation. That winter would be remembered for a desertion rate that averaged 200 men a day. Burnside was replaced by "Fighting Joe" Hooker, who was successful in restoring morale, but whose shortcomings as a commander were cruelly exploited by Lee at Chancellorsville in May 1863.

After that, Lee moved audaciously to invade the North. General George Meade relieved Hooker and took over the Army of the Potomac in time to turn Lee back in the Battle of Gettysburg on July 3. But Meade too failed to pursue the retreating rebels, and his ensuing campaigns were inconclusive. It wasn't until Lincoln plucked Ulysses S. Grant from his Western command that he found a general both brilliant and dogged enough to win the war.

Once deprived of command, McClellan saw an alternate route to his goal of preserving the Union and accepted the Democrats' presidential nomination in 1864. The Union, he was convinced, was in as much danger from radical Republicans as from Confederate armies. In late August, when the Democratic Convention opened in Chicago, it was widely believed he would win the November election. Lincoln wrote privately, "This morning, as for some days past, it seems exceedingly probable that this Administration will not be re-elected."

The situation changed dramatically between McClellan's nomination and Election Day. Northern victories at Atlanta and in the Shenandoah Valley turned the war from an issue favoring the

Democrats to a Republican asset. The Democratic Party platform called for an immediate end to hostilities and settlement with the Confederates. But there was a rift: McClellan believed peace talks should be pursued only after the South agreed to reunion, putting him at odds with his party and the candidate it chose as his running mate, Ohio Senator George H. Pendleton.

Republican orators, pamphlet writers, and cartoonists seized on the contradiction - depicting the Democrats as the party of disloyalty and McClellan as an advocate of peace at any price. Political strategists had assumed that if General McClellan ran, he would sweep the military vote. But the soldiers' enthusiasm was extinguished by the Democratic peace platform. In the North as a whole, Lincoln captured 55 percent of the vote, but 78 percent of the troops backed him. Even in the Army of the Potomac, McClellan's army, just three of ten voters cast ballots for their old commander. One newspaper cartoon showed a soldier observing McClellan with his political allies: "Good bye 'little Mac,'" the caption read, "if that's your company, Uncle Abe gets my vote."

After the election, McClellan sailed for Europe and more than three years of self-imposed exile, remaining abroad through the war's closing scenes and the beginning of the Reconstruction era. Talk of another presidential campaign in 1868 was abandoned after the Republicans nominated General Grant; few Democrats, a newspaper reported, were enthusiastic at the thought of "running the man who didn't take Richmond against the man who did."

In 1877, Democrats in McClellan's home state of New Jersey nominated him for governor, which came as a surprise because he had not expressed interest in the position. He was elected, and served a single term, which expired in 1881. Three years later, he backed Grover Cleveland's successful campaign for president of the United States but was blocked from his expected appointment as secretary of war. He spent his later years making a comfortable living as an engineering consultant and railroad executive.

In the writing he did on the Civil War during this time, his illusions remained intact. A half-finished manuscript on the events of his wartime command was found on his desk when he died suddenly of heart failure in 1885. His final thoughts had been of his beloved Army of the Potomac. He pictured the scene in July 1862 on the Peninsula, where his dream of victory had been shattered. As he imagined it, his army was "still proud and defiant, and strong in the consciousness of a great feat of arms heroically accomplished." It was an episode to "dignify a nation's history," a fit subject "for the grandest efforts of the poet and the painter." No sense of failure intruded on the memory; whatever had happened, it was not his fault.

4
THE TRIAL OF
JOHN BROWN
– THOMAS FLEMING

The court clerk droned on while the tall, bearded man and his four allies stood before the bench. Few men, according to one reporter, could look John Brown in the eye for more than a moment. But Judge Richard Parker asked Brown how he pleaded to the grand jury's accusations of treason, servile insurrection, and murder.

Brown replied, "Not guilty," then lay down on a cot, drew a blanket up to his chin, and closed his eyes. The trial that would inflame a nation had begun.

The country courtroom's whitewashed walls were smeared with haphazard fingerprints, the floor littered with peanut and chestnut shells. The benches on three sides of the courtroom were crammed with as many as 600 spectators. Outside in the streets of Charlestown, Virginia, several thousand more people were held at bay by lines of militiamen.

At the lawyers' table, Andrew Hunter, special counsel for the Commonwealth of Virginia, sat alongside Charles Harding, Jefferson County's regular prosecutor. A notorious drunk, Harding wore a stained coat, his hair was uncombed, and stubble covered his chin. On the other side, representing the defense, were Lawson Botts, and Thomas C. Green, the mayor of Charlestown. But all eyes were on Brown, whose fanatic daring had created this epic drama.

An undeniable power could emanate from John Brown when he chose to unleash it. The spectators had gotten a glimpse of it the day before, when the sheriff brought Brown and his confederates into the courtroom to be arraigned before eight justices of the peace for the grand jury hearing. Brown had walked from the nearby jail, head erect, stride steady. Prosecutor Harding, in charge of the arraignment, asked if the defendants had counsel, or if they wished the court to assign them qualified lawyers. Brown rose, and in a low, intense voice that reached every corner of the courtroom, struck the first blow in his own defense:

"Virginians, I did not ask for any quarter at the time

I was taken. I did not ask to have my life spared. The governor of the state of Virginia tendered me his assurance that I should have a fair trial. But, under no circumstances whatever will I be able to have a fair trial. If you seek my blood, you can have it at any moment, without this mockery of a trial. I have had no counsel. I have not been able to advise with anyone. I know nothing about the feelings of my fellow prisoners, and am utterly unable to attend in any way to my own defense. My memory don't serve me. My health is insufficient, although improving. There are mitigating circumstances that I would urge in our favor, if a fair trial is to be allowed us. But if we are to be forced with a mere form — a trial for execution — you might spare yourselves that trouble. I am ready for my fate. . . . I have now little further to ask, other than that I may not be foolishly insulted only as cowardly barbarians insult those who fall into their power."

From boyhood, Brown had faith that he was destined for great things. But before 1855, his life was mostly a series of bankruptcies and lawsuits. He married twice and had twenty children, only eleven of which survived to adulthood.

Although he did little about it in a practical sense, he hated slavery. His abolitionist views earned him a visit in 1846 from Frederick Douglass, the ex-slave who had become a well-known lecturer in the North. Brown, at the time, was working as a wool merchant. Douglass, who believed slavery could be abolished peacefully, was alarmed by Brown's declaration that "no political action will ever abolish the system of slavery. It will have to go out in blood. Those men who hold slaves have even forfeited their right to live."

When the wool business failed, Brown persuaded philanthropist Gerrit Smith to give him a portion of the 120,000 acres in upstate New York that Smith had opened to black refugees. There, Brown lived as a farmer and stern head of household to the handful of blacks who took advantage of Smith's hospitality.

Brown found his calling in Kansas. Five of his sons had gone west in search of land and opportunity, and landed instead in a cauldron of North-South animosity. Brown responded to his sons' call for help by abandoning the New York farm and joining them as "Captain" Brown, a title chosen in memory of his ancestor, who had died of illness in 1776 while serving in the Revolutionary Army.

Brown swiftly revealed a talent for guerrilla warfare. On May 24-25, 1856, he led his sons and a few followers in a raid on a handful of pro-southern settlers living on Pottawatomie Creek. The raiders dragged five people, including the father and two oldest sons of the Doyle family, out of their homes and murdered them. The slaughter - several of the victims were hacked almost to pieces by sabers -

caused such a general revulsion that Brown and his sons had to flee. James Redpath, an ardently abolitionist reporter, found Brown hiding in a Kansas creek bed and interviewed him for an article in which Brown declared he had nothing to do with the Pottawatomie murders, although he "approved of them" as reprisal for murders committed by the pro-slavers.

The propaganda - plus his courage in several Kansas skirmishes, particularly the battle at Osawatomie against proslavery forces - made Brown a hero to a small circle of abolitionists who advocated violence to overthrow slavery. This popularity helped Brown finance a slave-and-horse-stealing expedition into Missouri, and eventually launch what was covertly referred to as "the well-matured plan."

This was the attack on Harpers Ferry, which Brown led on Sunday, October 16, 1859. With twenty-one armed followers, he seized the federal arsenal just across the Potomac River from Maryland and converted it into a fortress to which, Brown was confident, every slave in the area would flee. The next day, a Virginia militia drove Brown and his band out of the arsenal and into the adjacent fire-engine house. A furious fire fight raged for the next day and a half, until all but seven of the raiders were killed, captured, or dispersed.

Brown tried to leverage ten local white hostages for safe passage into the Maryland hills, but U.S.

Army Colonel Robert E. Lee, ordered to the scene by President Buchanan, declined to bargain. When Brown refused a final demand to surrender, Lee sent a dozen Marines, led by Lieutenant Israel Green, crashing through the engine-room door with fixed bayonets. Green, according to his own account, caught Brown as he was reloading his gun and beat him to the ground with repeated blows to the head from his light dress sword.

Later, lying on the floor of the office of the armory paymaster, Brown was confronted by Virginia Governor Henry A. Wise and interrogated for more than three hours. His plan had failed, Brown insisted, because he had neglected tactics out of humane consideration for the hostages. He lamented that his wounds were inflicted "some minutes after I had ceased fighting and had consented to a surrender for the benefit of others, not for my own."

Brown said he could have killed Lieutenant Green, "but I supposed he came in only to receive our surrender." When it was pointed out that the lieutenant had scrambled headfirst through an opening battered in the door, with bullets whistling all around him, and that the first man to follow him had been killed and the second seriously wounded, Brown solemnly explained that the Marines had fired first. This was another lie; the Marines had strict orders to use only their bayonets to avoid harming the hostages.

The nation was shocked by initial reports, based on rumors, of a military invasion and an uprising involving thousands of slaves. When the true dimensions of Brown's futile foray became known, the reaction was bewilderment. Editors of the Cleveland *Leader* thought the whole affair was "positively ridiculous." The New York *Tribune* called it "the work of a madman." Even the *Liberator*, Boston's abolitionist organ, called the raid a "misguided, wild and apparently insane, though disinterested and well-intended effort by insurrection to emancipate the slaves." The Richmond *Inquirer* echoed most of the South when it declared, "The Harpers Ferry invasion has advanced the cause of Disunion more than any other event that has happened since the formation of the Government."

The reference in the indictment to "divers other evil-minded and traitorous persons to the Jurors unknown" fed rumors of a conspiracy, soon supported by evidence. On a Maryland farm a few miles from Harpers Ferry, where Brown had spent the summer planning the raid, investigators found a carpetbag full of correspondence between Brown and his backers. Many of the primary investors in Brown's scheme vanished. Frederick Douglass and several others left for Canada, beyond the reach of federal warrants. Gerrit Smith had a mental breakdown and was confined to an asylum.

Within a week of his capture, Brown was on trial - in accordance with the Virginia statute, which required "when an indictment is found against a person for felony . . . the accused, if in custody, shall, unless good cause be shown for a continuance, be arraigned and tried in the same term." Governor Wise rejected the advice of some Virginians to declare martial law, convict Brown in a drumhead court, and hang him on the spot. He insisted the honor and reputation of the South made it imperative to give Brown every benefit the law allowed. Neither Wise nor his prosecutor could see that they were dueling John Brown for the minds and hearts of millions of neutral northerners.

Already, Brown's tactics were having their effect beyond the borders of Virginia. The Lawrence, Kansas, *Republican* fulminated, "We defy an instance to be shown in a civilized community where a prisoner has been forced to trial for his life, when so disabled by sickness or ghastly wounds as to be unable even to sit up during the proceedings, and compelled to be carried to the judgment hall upon a litter." But Brown did not convince everyone. The reporter for the *New York Tribune* wrote, "The prisoner . . . is evidently not much injured, but is determined to resist the pushing of his trial by all the means in his power."

Brown was skilled at putting his accusers on the defensive. But he had more practical reasons to delay. He had sent letters north to three prominent lawyers; as yet, none had responded. Moreover, if he managed to stall long enough, his supporters might have time to mount a rescue operation; freeing prisoners from well-guarded jails had been done more than once in Kansas.

When news of the trial reached Boston, abolitionist John W. Le Barnes hired George H. Hoyt, a fledgling lawyer who was only twenty-one (and looked nineteen), to leave immediately for Charlestown. Hoyt was to watch and report on the proceedings, talk with Brown and deliver any messages he might have to his friends. Secondly, he was instructed to send Barnes "an accurate and detailed account of the military situation at Charlestown, the number and distribution of troops, the location and defenses of the jail, and nature of the approaches to the town and jail, the opportunities for a sudden attack, and the means of retreat, with the location and situation of the room in which Brown is confined, and all other particulars that might enable friends to consult as to some plan of attempt at rescue."

Hoyt was riding a southbound train when Brown resumed his cot for the second day of his trial. The defense presented a telegram received late the previous night from Akron, Ohio, testifying that insanity was hereditary in the Brown family. Before either prosecuting attorney could object, Brown did: "As I remarked to Mr. Green, insane persons, so far as my experience goes, have but little ability to judge of their own sanity; and if I am insane, of course I should think I know more than all the rest of the world. But I do not think so. I am perfectly unconscious of insanity, and I reject, so far as I am capable, any attempt to interfere in my behalf on that score."

The defendant's abashed lawyers dropped the plea. But they promptly presented the court with another document: a telegram from Judge Daniel Tilden, announcing he was en route from Ohio in response to Brown's letter. Botts and Green requested a delay until Tilden arrived.

The prosecutors objected; Hunter asked tartly if Tilden was a lawyer or a leader of a band of desperadoes, and insisted that if additional lawyers were coming, more than enough time had elapsed for them to reach Charlestown. What was there to debate, really? Brown had admitted and even gloried in his crimes.

Green lumbered to his feet in sharp rebuttal. Treason, he argued, could be confessed only in open court. What Brown had said to one or even 100 persons outside the court was irrelevant. Equally "idle," Green said, were the prosecutor's fears of a rescue attempt. Earnestly, Green asked Judge Parker for only one day's delay, but the motion was denied.

In the defense's opening statement, Lawson Botts argued that Virginia had no right to try Brown. To convict Brown of premeditated murder, Botts said, the prosecution must present evidence of malice, and Brown had gone to great lengths to guarantee the safety of the prisoners he had taken. Botts contended the charge of treason was invalid because, according to common-law tradition in the United States, treason could be committed only by a resident against his own state, and no stretch of logic could make Brown a citizen of Virginia. Finally, Botts questioned the court's jurisdiction over crimes committed on federal property such as an arsenal.

Hunter replied with obvious pride that the Virginia law on treason was "more full" than the federal statute. A person was guilty of treason not only if he levied war against Virginia or gave aid to its enemies, but also if he established without the authority of the legislature "any governments within its limits separate from the existing government." As for jurisdiction, Hunter cited an 1830 case involving a murder committed on the arsenal grounds, in which the killer had been tried, convicted, and executed under Virginia laws.

The prosecution produced witnesses who gave a detailed narration of the assault on Harpers Ferry. A. J. Phelps, a conductor with the Baltimore & Ohio Railroad, testified that when his train arrived at the bridge outside Harpers Ferry shortly after midnight Sunday, he was warned by a wounded bridge watchman that riflemen had seized the arsenal. The conductor refused to take his train into Harpers Ferry. The station's baggage master, a freed black man named Hayward Shepherd, walked out on the bridge to ask what was wrong, and was struck in the back by a bullet fired from the armory gate. Twelve hours later, Shepherd died in agony on the floor of the railroad station while the battle raged around the arsenal.

Phelps testified that he returned to Harpers Ferry two days after the raid with Governor Wise and heard John Brown describe books that he said explained everything. Lee, who had confiscated one of the books, gave it to the governor. Brown explained it was the constitution of a "provisional government" in which he was president and commander-in-chief. Brown said there was also a secretary of state, a secretary of war, and all the other officers for a general government, including a house of representatives which included "an intelligent colored man."

Green interrupted the "sensational" testimony to ask the court once more for a delay. He had received a message that counsel was arriving from Cleveland and would almost certainly be there by nightfall. The prosecution had selected "only scraps" of Brown's long conversation with

Governor Wise, Green said, and the new counsel should have an opportunity to cross-examine the witness. Hunter answered that other witnesses would cover much of the same ground, and the new counsel – if he arrived – would have ample opportunities to question them.

The judge ordered the testimony to proceed, and Green got Phelps to admit that Brown had said on Sunday night "it was not his intention to harm anybody or anything. He was sorry men had been killed. It was not by his orders or with his approbation."

Colonel Lewis Washington took the stand next. The most distinguished of Brown's hostages, he bore a striking resemblance to his famous great-granduncle, President George Washington. The colonel testified that four of Brown's lieutenants had woken him between 1:00 and 2:00 a.m. and at gunpoint ordered him and his slaves to come with them to Harpers Ferry. The raiders forced the colonel to hand over an old dress sword allegedly presented by Frederick the Great to George Washington. Later, the colonel was astonished to see the relic in Brown's hands. "I will take especial care of it and I shall endeavor to return it to you after you are released," Brown told him. Brown carried the sword throughout the battle and put it aside only when the Marines began to batter down the door.

Brown told each of the hostages that he could ransom himself by summoning a "stout Negro" to take his place, which Washington and the others declined to do. The colonel testified: "No Negro from this neighborhood appeared to take arms voluntarily."

Not long after the court adjourned, George Hoyt arrived from Boston. Hunter took one look at him and wrote to Governor Wise, "A beardless boy came in last night as Brown's counsel. I think he is a spy." The next morning when Hoyt appeared in court, Hunter demanded proof that he was a member of the Boston bar. Northern newspapers, unaware of Hoyt's real mission, were enraged. Embarrassed, Hoyt murmured that he had brought no credentials. Judge Parker said he would accept "any citizen's evidence" that Hoyt was a qualified attorney. Green said he had read letters from Hoyt's fellow students alluding to him as a member of the bar. That was enough; the Judge permitted Hoyt to take the oath and his seat beside Bolts and Green.

Hunter paraded more witnesses to the stand. Armsted Ball, a master machinist who worked at the Harpers Ferry armory, testified he was seized by Brown's men when he went to the arsenal to investigate the disturbance. Ball said he prevented one of Brown's men from firing at an old man named Guess who was passing by, but was unable to stop him from killing Harpers Ferry Mayor

Fontaine Beckham, who had ventured onto the railroad trestle to get a better look at the excitement in the arsenal below.

Four other witnesses were called in quick succession during the afternoon session, and the prosecution – convinced it had made its case against Brown – rested.

The first defense witness, a hostage named Joseph Brewer, described the strange mixture of murder and mercy that characterized the bloodshed at Harpers Ferry. He testified that when Brown sent his lieutenant, Aaron Stevens, and hostage A. M. Kitzmiller out with a flag of truce, the maddened citizens of Harpers Ferry riddled Stevens with bullets. Brewer, realizing Stevens was still alive, risked his life to carry the wounded man into a nearby building. Then, fulfilling a pledge he had made to Brown, Brewer returned to the engine house. Both he and Kitzmiller, who testified next, said Brown urged them to use their influence with the citizens to prevent unnecessary bloodshed.

Green asked Judge Parker for permission to introduce testimony about the death of one of Brown's raiders, William Thompson, who was seized by the militia as he left the engine house to negotiate a truce. Hunter objected; all this testimony about Brown's forbearance, he insisted, had no more to do with the legal realities of the case than the "dead languages." But the judge ruled the evidence admissible, and Hunter had to sit stolidly while his own son, Harry, recited a grisly tale: "After Mr. Beckham, who was my granduncle, was shot, I was much exasperated and started with Mr. Chambers to the room where . . . Thompson was confined, with the purpose of shooting him. . . . We then caught hold of him, and dragged him out by the throat, he saying, 'though you may take my life, 80,000 will rise up to avenge me and carry out my purpose of giving liberty to the slaves.' We carried him out to the bridge and the two of us, leveling our guns in this moment of wild exasperation fired, and before he fell, a dozen or more balls were buried in him; we then threw his body off the trestlework. . . . I had just seen my loved uncle and best friend I ever had, shot down by those villainous Abolitionists, and felt justified in shooting any that I could find; I felt it my duty, and I have no regrets."

The defense summoned several more witnesses, but none were present to take the stand. Brown suddenly rose from his cot to protest: "I discover that notwithstanding all the assurances I have received of a fair trial, nothing like a fair trial is to be given me, as it would seem. I gave the names, as soon as I could get them, of the persons I wished to have called as witnesses, and was assured that they would be subpoenaed. I wrote down a memorandum to that effect, saying where those parties were; but it appears they have not been subpoenaed as far as I can learn; and I now ask, if I am to have anything at all deserving the name and shadow of a fair trial, that this proceeding be deferred until tomorrow morning; for I have no counsel, as I before stated, in whom I feel that I can rely, but I am in hopes counsel may arrive who will attend to seeing that I get the witnesses who are necessary for my defense."

Reporting this outburst, the *New York Herald's* correspondent said, "The indignation of the citizens scarcely knew bounds. He [Brown] was stigmatized as an ungrateful villain, and some declared he deserved hanging for that act alone." The sheriff assured Judge Parker that all Brown's subpoenas had been served, and the courtroom seethed. Brown lay down again, drew his blanket over him, and closing his eyes, "appeared to sink in tranquil slumber."

Hoyt, too, pleaded for a delay. He knew that Brown's explosive repudiation of his court-appointed counsel meant that he was about to be left with the full responsibility for the defense. Hoyt told Judge Parker he had not even read the indictment and did not have "any idea of the line of the defense proposed . . ." or "knowledge of the criminal code of Virginia and no time to read it." Botts offered Hoyt the full resources of his law office and declared he would "sit up with him all night to put him in possession of all the law and facts in relation to this case." Reluctantly, Judge Parker agreed to a brief postponement and adjourned at 6:00 p.m.

Botts spent the night tutoring Hoyt in Virginia criminal law, only to discover in the morning that it was unnecessary. Two experienced lawyers had at last arrived in response to Brown's call for counsel. Hiram Griswold of Cleveland had been sent by Judge Tilden; and Samuel Chilton, a Virginian by birth, had been hired (for a fee of $1,000) by John A. Andrew, a leading Boston abolitionist. Chilton asked Judge Parker for a few hours to prepare. But Parker, weary of pleas for delay, declared Brown had no one to blame but himself for dismissing his previous counsel.

Hoyt summoned more of the hostages, who added only grim details to the overall picture, such as seeing two of Brown's sons fatally wounded during the first day's fighting. Hunter charged the defense with calculating a course to waste time. Hoyt said he was trying to "prove the absence of malicious intention," and was acting in accordance "with the express commands" of his client. Hunter gave up and allowed the parade of witnesses to continue, but did not bother to cross-examine them.

By the time the court adjourned for a one-hour recess, the defense had run out of witnesses. It was Saturday, and Judge Parker was determined to end the trial before nightfall. But Brown was equally determined to prolong it until Monday. When the bailiffs summoned him to reappear in court, Brown again said he was too sick to rise from his jail bed. The Judge demanded a report from the doctor, who said Brown was malingering. Parker ordered Brown carried into court, but another hour had been consumed.

Chilton asked the judge to compel the prosecutors to elect one count of the indictment and abandon the others, arguing it was unfair to force Brown to defend himself against three accusations simultaneously. But Parker ruled the jury had been charged and sworn to try the prisoners on the indictment as drawn. The trial must go on, but Chilton could at its close ask for "an arrest of judgment."

All that was left was for the two sides to make closing arguments. Griswold asked for an adjournment after the prosecution had completed its statements so that he and Chilton could make a more respectable defense on Monday morning. Once more, there was a wrangle over this request for delay. Hunter blamed Brown for "dismissing his faithful, skillful, able and zealous counsel yesterday afternoon," and could see no reason why the jurors should be kept away from their families for the weekend. Chilton said he hoped the court would not require a man on trial for his life to submit his case without an adequate argument. Judge Parker reluctantly agreed.

Pulling himself out of his alcoholic fog, the county prosecutor declaimed for about forty minutes while Hunter squirmed in his chair. "When Harding began to speak," recalled one of the spectators, "if you shut your eyes and listened, for the first few minutes you would think Patrick Henry had returned to earth; after that he dwindled away into ineptitudes." After Harding's harangue, Parker adjourned the court until 9:00 a.m. Monday.

The judge and Hunter could only glare in chagrin as John Brown, rose from his cot the moment the gavel fell and walked back to his cell.

On Monday, Griswold and Chilton spoke in Brown's defense, but Botts had already made the best available arguments, and the lawyers did little more than paraphrase him. They maintained that Brown was not a Virginia citizen, the court did not have jurisdiction over the federal arsenal, and Brown's consideration to his hostages proved his lack of malice and, therefore, his innocence of first-degree murder.

In reply, prosecutor Hunter explained to the jury that anyone who killed while committing a felony was guilty of first-degree murder. He argued Virginia code defined citizens as all white persons born in any other state who became residents, and Brown was attempting to become a resident, albeit a most unwelcome one, when he seized the arsenal. He had come to stay, Hunter said, "for the nefarious purpose of rallying forces into this Commonwealth and establishing himself at Harpers Ferry as a starting point for a new Government." Brown's conduct, Hunter added, showed clearly that his raid was not intended to carry off slaves, and his provisional government was "a real thing and no debating society." His treatment of the prisoners was meant to lull the citizens of Virginia into letting him "usurp the government, manumit our slaves, confiscate the property of slave holders and, without drawing a trigger or shedding blood, permit him to take possession of the Commonwealth." Hunter asked that Brown be convicted so that "the majesty of the laws" might be vindicated.

Throughout these orations, Brown lay on his back with his eyes closed. Chilton asked Judge Parker to instruct the jury that they could not convict Brown of treason, but Parker denied the motion. Chilton asked the judge to rule on the question of jurisdiction. Parker affirmed the court's jurisdiction, and the jury retired. For three-quarters of an hour, the court was in recess. Then the spectators swarmed back to hear the foreman of the jury announce that John Brown had been found guilty on all counts. There was not a sound in the courtroom.

Chilton moved for an arrest of judgment, citing the well-debated errors in the indictment. Parker promised to hear arguments on it the following day, and the court adjourned after selecting a jury to try Brown follower Edwin Coppoc.

When Parker arrived in court on Wednesday, the jury had already been seated for Coppoc's trial; his ruling on Chilton's motion would have to wait. Once Coppoc's guilt was confirmed that afternoon, Parker summoned Brown to the courtroom and struck down the motion for an arrest of judgment. Then the clerk asked Brown, still prone on his cot, whether he wished to say anything before the sentence was pronounced.

Brown was flustered; he expected that he and his confederates would be sentenced together. "I have, may it please the court," he said hesitantly, "a few words to say." He braced himself, seeming to realize that he was a dead man. The law had condemned him, and he no longer needed to worry about arguments that satisfied judge and jury. In a voice that was to echo down bitter decades, John Brown spoke to America: "In the first place, I deny everything but what I have all along admitted: the design on my part to free slaves. . . . I never did intend murder, or treason, or the destruction of property, or to excite or incite slaves to rebellion, or to make insurrection. . . . Now, if it is deemed necessary that I should forfeit my life for the furtherance of the ends of justice, and mingle my blood further with the blood of my children and with the blood of millions in this slave country whose rights are disregarded by wicked, cruel, and unjust enactments, I submit; so let it be done!"

Brown added about his followers: "I hear it has been stated by some of them that I have induced them to join me. But the contrary is true. I do not say this to injure them, but as regretting their weakness. There is not one of them but joined me of his own accord, and the greater part of them at their own expense. A number of them I never saw, and never had a word of conversation with, till the day they came to me; and that was for the purpose I have stated."

Of course, Brown was lying about his followers. Two weeks before the attack, one of the younger raiders, William H. Leeman, wrote: "I am now in a Southern *Slave State* and before I leave it, it will be a *free state* . . ." Frederick Douglass later recalled watching John Brown run his finger down a map of the Alleghenies from the border of New York into the southern states. "These mountains," Brown said, "are the basis of my plan. God has given the strength of these hills to freedom; they were placed here to aid the emancipation of your race." Brown told Douglass he would create an armed force in "the very heart of the South," gathering and arming recruits from the slave population, keeping "the most restless and daring" in their ranks, and sending the others north.

On November 2, Judge Parker sentenced Brown to death by hanging, to be carried out precisely a month later. Letters poured into Governor Wise's office threatening, exhorting, and pleading with him not to hang John Brown. From Massachusetts, Amos Lawrence, who had given Brown money, warned the Governor, "From his blood would spring an army of martyrs." Fernando Wood, the pro-southern mayor of New York, wrote, "Dare you do a bold thing and temper justice with Mercy? Have you nerve enough to send Brown to the State Prison instead of hanging him?"

Many in the South were eager to see Brown die no matter the consequences. "Though it convert the whole Northern people, without an exception, into furious armed abolition invaders," the Richmond *Whig* declared, "Yet old Brown will be hung!"

The headstrong governor did not need advice from either side. Two days after Brown's sentence, he wrote to Fernando Wood: "My mind is inflexibly made up." He rejected the argument that the hanging would make Brown a martyr. He could see no difference, so far as martyrdom was concerned, between the noose and a life sentence in a Virginia prison.

Some of Brown's friends continued to foment desperate plans to free him. One involved gathering Kansas raiders and German immigrant volunteers to storm the jail some propitious midnight.

Another, even wilder scheme involved kidnapping Governor Wise and smuggling him aboard a seagoing tug, where he was to be held hostage until exchanged for Brown. None of the plots came close to fruition, in part because sensible men saw they were all but hopeless and declined to donate the thousands of dollars needed to set them in motion. More importantly, Brown did not want rescued; he accepted and even gloried in "being worth infinitely more now to die than to live."

Nerving himself for his final ordeal, Brown refused to see his wife until the day before his execution. In a letter to a cousin, he consoled himself that he had "never since I can remember required a great amount of sleep: so that I conclude that I have already enjoyed full an average amount of waking hours with those who reach their 'three scores and ten.'" The best of Brown's letters were reprinted in newspapers throughout the North. They reportedly brought tears to the eyes of his southern jailer as he read and sealed them.

Brown's lawyers asked the Virginia court of appeals to overturn his conviction based on the argument over jurisdiction. They were turned down.

On December 2, John Brown - wearing a black frock coat and pants, a black slouch hat, and red slippers - was led into the street by his guards and saw some 1,500 armed men deployed. "I had no idea that Governor Wise considered my execution so important," Brown gasped. Wise had, in fact, yielded to hysteria. He told President Buchanan that "Devils . . . trained in all the Indian arts of predatory war" were massing in Kansas and Ohio to rescue Brown. He persuaded the President to send Colonel Lee and 264 artillerymen to guard Harpers Ferry, and during the first two days of December, he clamped a security net around Charlestown which paralyzed the region. No one could travel on a train unless a station agent first issued a certificate of good character. Many people, including four congressmen, were jailed on suspicion the moment they reached Charlestown.

The day was clear and warm, and as Brown rode to the place of his execution, seated on his coffin in a wagon drawn by two white horses, he looked out at the Blue Ridge Mountains and said, "This is a beautiful country. I never truly had the pleasure of seeing it before." Around the gallows, there were few civilians; Governor Wise had issued a proclamation urging the citizens to stay home and guard their property.

Brown mounted the scaffold with unwavering steps, threw aside his hat, and stood still while the sheriff tied a noose and white hood around his neck.

Major Thomas Jackson, soon to be dubbed "Stonewall" attended the execution. In a letter to his wife, Jackson described how the sheriff severed the rope that held the tray door and "Brown fell through about five inches, his knees falling on a level with the position occupied by his feet before the rope was cut. With the fall his arms, below the elbows, flew up horizontally, his hands clinched; and his arms gradually fell, but by spasmodic motions. . . . Soon the wind blew his lifeless body to and fro. . . . I sent up a petition that he might be saved." Preston climbed the scaffold and thundered: "So perish all such enemies of Virginia! All such enemies of the Union! All such foes of the human race!"

Speaking in Kansas the same day, President Lincoln said, "Old John Brown has been executed for treason against a State. We cannot object, even though he agreed with us in thinking slavery wrong. That cannot excuse violence, bloodshed and treason. It could avail him nothing that he might think himself right." But the voices of moderation were lost in the shouts of extremists. Virginia Senator James M. Mason, author of the Fugitive Slave Act, fulminated: "John Brown's invasion was condemned [in the North] only because it failed." The Joint Committee of the General Assembly of Virginia declared, "The crimes of John Brown were neither more nor less than practical illustrations of the doctrines of the leaders of the Republican party."

A year and a half later, Governor Wise, out of office, inspired a detachment of Virginians to seize the same Harpers Ferry arsenal - an act of reckless violence which did much to help the secessionists carry the day in the Virginia Convention. Lawson Botts, who had defended Brown so ably, died a Confederate colonel in the Second Battle of Bull Run. His fellow attorney, Thomas Green, served as a private in Botts's regiment. Prosecutor Andrew Hunter emerged from the war a ruined man, his fine house burned by northern troops. Charles Harding, dissipated as he was, volunteered to serve his native state with a musket on his shoulder, and early in the war, died of pneumonia after a freezing night on picket duty.

On July 18, 1861, the 12th Massachusetts Regiment marched through the streets of Boston singing an improvised song about John Brown's body. Men from Ohio sang other versions of it as the nation plunged into four mad years of war. In his poem in praise of Harriet Beecher Stowe, wry Oliver Wendell Holmes perhaps best assayed John Brown's legacy:

> All through the conflict up and down
> Marched Uncle Tom and Old John Brown,
> One ghost, one form ideal.
> And which was false and which was true,
> And which was mightier of the two,
> The wisest sybil never knew,
> For both alike were real.

5
THE
UNKNOWABLE MAN
– STEPHEN W. SEARS

In 1905, on a visit to Richmond, author Henry James was struck by the sight of a statue of Robert E. Lee. There was, James thought, something in the figure suggesting "a quite sublime effort to ignore, to sit, as it were, superior and indifferent . . . so that the vast association of the futile for the moment drops away from it." Decades later, Lee's biographer Douglas Southall Freeman passed the statue every day and invariably saluted it. "I shall not fail to do that as long as I live," Freeman said.

Such is the paradox of the man that both those who consider Lee a detriment to the Confederacy and those who consider him a military genius reach the same conclusion: The South would have been better off without him. Detractors say Lee squandered the South's slim resources; admirers say that without Lee, the Confederacy would have crumbled early, thus saving numerous lives in both North and South.

Understanding Lee has never been a simple task. To poet Stephen Vincent Benét, Lee was:

> A figure lost to flesh and blood and bones,
>
> Frozen into a legend out of life,
>
> A blank-verse statue - . . .
>
> For here was someone who lived all his life
>
> In the most fierce and open light of the sun
>
> And kept his heart a secret to the end
>
> From all the picklocks of biographers.

Benét called him "the marble man."

In the aftershock of the surrender at Appomattox, most Southerners were not inclined to idolize their generals. The war had been lost, and there was nothing to celebrate except the end to the killing. But even then, Lee was the most respected of all the South's generals. In the years after the war, first in Richmond and then as president of Washington College in Lexington (now Washington and Lee), Lee was quietly honored by his fellow Virginians whenever they had the opportunity. During a modest military cortege after his death in Lexington in 1870, bells tolled, and a battery from the Virginia Military Institute fired minute guns. The general's last words had been "Strike the tent."

But that was not the end of his story. Creating the myth of Robert E. Lee began only after his death. In life, Lee did not possess false modesty; he was proud of what he had done. "There is nothing left me to do but to go and see General Grant," he had said on the day he surrendered at Appomattox, "and I would rather die a thousand deaths." Those who appointed him the marble man, however, were out of his reach. Historian C. Vann Woodward wrote that the creation of Lee's legend was "the work of many hands, not all of them pious, the product of mixed motives, not all of them worthy."

In *The Marble Man: Robert E. Lee and His Image in American Society,* Thomas L. Connelly chronicled the rise of what he termed the Lee cult. Two rival Lee factions, in Lexington and Richmond, coalesced within a decade, and by the end of the 1870s, were hard at work. Theirs was an all-Virginian operation - states' rights energized them as well as the Confederacy - brought to life by generals of the former Army of Northern Virginia: Jubal Early, William N. Pendleton, Fitzhugh Lee (Lee's nephew), Lee's former staff members Walter H. Taylor and Charles Marshall, and J. William Jones, a Baptist minister. The group's mission,

Connelly wrote, was to appropriate Robert E. Lee "as a balm to soothe defeat" and as the paladin of the lost cause. "To justify Lee was to justify the Southern cause."

Through speeches, articles, biographies, campaign narratives, and the Papers of the Southern Historical Society, cult members seized control of Confederate historiography and turned it to the production of Lee's sainthood. This veneration, explains Lee biographer Marshall Fishwick, created a Saint George of Virginia. To people in the South, going through Reconstruction, this depiction of Lee was truly a figure of worship.

Thomas Connelly saw considerable irony in the hagiographical efforts of the Lee cult. The general's "military greatness alone would have assured his niche as a major national figure," he wrote, without all the manipulation that went into creating the marble man. Later historians have sifted through everything Lee wrote to uncover the man behind the marble. At the same time, Lee's ideas, strategy, and tactics have been consistently reexamined anew in efforts to reinterpret his role in Confederate history.

The Lee who emerges is marked by more humanity and affected by more emotions than the demigod Lee. There can be little doubt, for example, that his youthful ambition to succeed and his sense of duty were inspired by stories about his father,

Henry Lee III, also known as Light-Horse Harry, a Revolutionary War hero who deserted his family when Lee was six years old.

Henry Lee, in addition to his military career, made his name in Virginia politics. As a delegate to the Congress of the Confederation, he had favored the adoption of the United States Constitution. While serving as Virginia's ninth governor, a new county – Lee – was named for him. After his election to the United States House of Representatives in 1799, he delivered a famous eulogy for his former general and president, George Washington, declaring him "first in war . . . first in peace . . . and first in the hearts of his countrymen." Robert Lee's mother, Anne Hill Carter, had grown up at Shirley Plantation, one of the most elegant homes in Virginia. It was there in 1793 that she married Henry, seventeen years her senior, and on January 19, 1807, gave birth to Robert.

When Lee was two, his father – unable to meet obligations on lands he had purchased, and banned by law from using his wife's inheritance – was sent to debtor's prison. When Henry was released in 1810, he moved the family to a small house in Alexandria, Virginia, where Anne had relatives. Two years later, during a political riot in Baltimore, Henry was badly beaten. Besides extensive internal injuries, his face and head were disfigured, and even his speech was affected. He went to the West Indies in 1813 to recuperate. Five years later, when Robert was eleven, Henry died on Cumberland Island, Georgia, as he was making his way back to Virginia.

In 1824, at the age of seventeen, Robert Lee won an appointment to the United States Military Academy at West Point, primarily on the recommendation of a relative, William Henry Fitzhugh. But due to a surfeit of cadets, he did not begin his studies there until 1825. He graduated second in his class in 1829 and was named a second lieutenant in the Army Corps of Engineers. He also married Mary Custis, and the couple had the first of their seven children, George Washington Custis Lee .

When the Mexican-American War broke out in 1846, Lee proved as adept at military strategy as he had been at mathematics. As one of General "Old Fuss and Feathers" Winfield Scott's chief aides in the march to Mexico City, Lee found routes of attack that the Mexicans had not defended because they thought the terrain impassable. He was wounded at the Battle of Chapultepec, where he fought alongside Ulysses S. Grant. His performance during the Mexican-American War led to promotions – first to major, then lieutenant colonel and colonel, the rank he held at the outbreak of the Civil War in 1861.

No doubt the slack pace of promotion in the antebellum Army caused Lee to question his career in the military. In the thirteen years between wars, Lee juggled management of a plantation in Arlington, which he inherited after the death of his father-in-law George Washington Parke Custis, a tenure as superintendent of the Military Academy at West Point, and command of the Second Calvary regiment in Texas.

Lee complained about the seemingly endless separations from wife and family during his service in the Army. Mary suffered from rheumatoid arthritis, which eventually confined her to a wheelchair.

Lee was reserved, moody, and prone to hypochondria. Despite his complaints, he threw himself into his Army career.

Lee was conflicted on the issue of slavery. He spent little time on his Virginia plantation, where Mary taught female slaves to read and write. Though she never freed her slaves, Mary was an advocate of eventual emancipation. Lee, according to biographer Douglas Freeman, held the prevailing view of religious people in the border states that "slavery existed because God willed it and . . . it would end when God so ruled."

In 1856, Lee wrote Mary that "slavery as an institution is a moral & political evil in any Country." But he believed that blacks were better off as slaves in America than free in Africa. "The painful discipline they are undergoing is necessary for their instruction as a race & I hope it will prepare & lead them to better things," he wrote, adding, "how long their subjugation may be necessary is known & ordered by a wise Merciful Providence."

When, hoping to incite a slave rebellion, Ohio abolitionist John Brown and twenty-one followers seized the federal arsenal at Harpers Ferry in 1859, Lee commanded the forces sent by Buchanan to suppress it. After three minutes of fighting, Lee reclaimed the fort and captured Brown, describing him in his report as "a fanatic or madman."

When the Southern states began to consider secession in the winter of 1860, Lee denounced the tactic as a "revolution" and betrayal of the efforts of the Founding Fathers. In early 1861, he wrote to his son, William Fitzhugh, that he could "anticipate no greater calamity for the country than a dissolution of the Union." He was in San Antonio when Texas voted to secede and was among the 4,000 U.S. Army soldiers who were forced to surrender. "Has it come so soon as this?" he asked as he returned to Washington, where Buchanan would appoint him colonel of the First Regiment of Cavalry.

Despite his increasing stature on the national stage, Lee remained devoted to his home state – and this, to him, trumped loyalty to the nation. "If Virginia stands by the old Union," he wrote a friend, "so will I. But if she secedes (though I do not believe in secession as a constitutional right, nor that there is sufficient cause for revolution), then I will follow my native State with my sword, and, if need be, with my life."

The people of Virginia were still undecided a month after seven states - Alabama, Florida, Georgia, Louisiana, Mississippi, South Carolina, and Texas – formed the Confederacy. On April 4, delegates to a convention voted down, by a two-to-one margin, a call for Virginia to secede. But the convention remained open, and the debate continued. On April 12, Confederate soldiers led by Brigadier General P. G. T. Beauregard seized control of Fort Sumter in South Carolina. President Abraham Lincoln, a month after his inauguration, responded by ordering a call-up of troops from states still loyal to the Union. Virginia was to supply three regiments of 2,340 men to march south and reclaim federal property. The Virginia delegates voted again on April 17 on a secession proposal; this time, the result was two-to-one in favor.

Three days later, when the news of Virginia's secession reached Lee in Washington, he resigned from the army. He had rejected Lincoln's offer of a senior command position, with the rank of major general. "Well, Mary," Lee said to his wife, "the question is settled." Lee had told one of his lieutenants, who asked if he would fight for the Union or the Confederacy, "I shall never bear arms against the Union, but it may be necessary for me to carry a musket in the defense of my native state, Virginia, in which case I shall not prove recreant to my duty." That time had come. Lee's decision astounded many of his friends and family, including his cousin, Rear Admiral Samuel Phillips Lee, who along with 40 percent of Virginian officers remained loyal to the Union.

On April 23, Lee took command of the Virginia army. Though he was designated one of the Confederacy's first five generals, he refused to wear the insignia of his rank until the war had been won, and he could be promoted in peacetime. Instead, he had the three stars of a Confederate colonel on his uniform. In early May, he wrote to Mary that "war is inevitable, and there is no telling when it will burst around you." He told her to evacuate their home outside Washington, the Custis Mansion (now the Robert E. Lee Memorial at Arlington National Cemetery), saying, "May God keep and preserve you and have mercy on all our people."

Early in the war, Lee's role was largely defensive. Assigned to organize Carolina and Georgia coastal defenses, he built up Fort Jackson and added two batteries that blocked any Union advance on Savannah. But then, after a 112-day siege, Union forces captured Fort Pulaski, near the mouth of the Savannah River, effectively closing Savannah as a strategic port. Despite being blamed for the setbacks, Lee was called back to Richmond and appointed military adviser to Jefferson Davis. He ordered trenches dug around the capitol in Richmond, for which he was ridiculed as the King of Spades. Lee's men called him Granny Lee because of his timid leadership style, and when he assumed control of the Army of Northern Virginia on June 1, 1862, Confederate newspaper editors objected, believing he would wait for the Union army to come to him.

The corollary to his battlefield self-confidence is equally important when it comes to understanding Robert E. Lee the soldier: He fought to win. Not every Civil War general fought that way. The Union army's Henry W. Halleck, for example, was primarily interested in gaining territory; George B. McClellan was notorious for finding ways not to fight; Joseph E. Johnston consistently retreated to avoid defeat.

Lee's critics T. Harry Williams and J. F. C. Fuller charge him with being overly aggressive and interested only in the Virginia theater of war; Williams called him "the last of the great old-fashioned generals." In fact, Lee was not old-fashioned.

Southerners, Lee believed, might win the war with the help of foreign intervention, as their forefathers had won the Revolution. Militarily, the best the Confederacy could hope on the Western front was to stop the Union advance there and gain a stalemate. Leaders of the Confederacy felt they could win their independence with a single major victory in the East. The destruction of the Union's principal army and guardian of Washington, the Army of the Potomac, at Sharpsburg or Gettysburg or perhaps Washington itself, offered the best chance to force Lincoln to negotiate for peace and the South's return to the Union with its "rights," including slavery, intact.

Lee disagreed. While he saw the advantages of British and French intervention, he was reluctant to rely on it. "We must make up our minds to fight our battles ourselves," he wrote in December 1861. "Expect to receive aid from no one. . . . The cry is too much for help." One of the general's staff members wrote that "since the whole duty of the nation would be war until independence should be secured, the whole nation should for the time be converted into an army, the producers to feed and the soldiers to fight." To this end, Lee endorsed a Confederacy-wide draft. The Confederate Congress passed a conscription bill in April 1862.

Lee forced the enemy to march to his drum – a tremendous accomplishment, especially since his was always the smaller army. At every opportunity, he seized the strategic initiative, as he did when taking field command for the first time during the Peninsula Campaign to beat back McClellan's

Army of the Potomac from taking Richmond in June 1862.

Connelly speculated that the various pressures on Lee's psyche produced a repressed personality, making Lee overly audacious and aggressive on the battlefield. The Confederate newspapers reversed their opinion of Lee after he drove Union forces from Richmond in the Seven Days' Battles of late June and early July 1862. Six battles – from Oak Grove to Malvern Hill – ended with McClellan in retreat and nearly 16,000 of his men dead. But the cost to the Confederacy had also been great; Lee's army suffered more than 20,000 casualties.

In fighting McClellan for Richmond, Lee took the offensive tactically as well as strategically. To remain on the defensive would have allowed McClellan to besiege Richmond, and to lose Richmond was a blow the Confederacy could not have survived. In any event, Lee's offensive was relentless, and his opponent gave way. This was also McClellan's first field command, and he broke under the pressure of the attack. Lee took note of that lesson.

The Second Bull Run (Second Manassas, in Southern terminology) campaign in August 1862 demonstrated how well Lee had learned the lessons of tactical command during the Seven Days' Battle. At Manassas, Lee commanded two flanks, led by major generals Thomas J. Stonewall Jackson and James Longstreet. Demonstrating an unerring sense of timing, the Confederates broke Union Major General John Pope's army before McClellan's forces could join it to overwhelm him. Lee was calm. When asked if he was worried that his advance force, under Jackson, might be destroyed before he came up with the rest of the army, he replied, "Not at all. I knew he [Stonewall] could hold on till we came, and that we should be in position in time."

Lee's decision to cross his country's northern frontier (as he called the Potomac) after the victory at Second Manassas and march into Maryland toward Pennsylvania has been much debated. Was it intended as an invasion? A raid? What could he hope to gain by changing the Confederacy's posture from defensive to offensive? Lee's rationale was straightforward: Crossing the Potomac was the only way to retain the initiative, and marching north offered the best way toward victory. McClellan, he had learned, was again his opponent, and he considered the Union officer "an able general but a very timid one." Looking back on the campaign, Lee said, "I went into Maryland to give battle," and had all gone as intended, "I would have fought and crushed him."

All did not go as Lee intended. A courier lost a copy of his campaign plan, and it was found by a Yankee soldier and brought to McClellan. The consequence was first the Battle of South

Mountain, where Lee succeeded only in buying time to reunite his divided army, and then the Battle of Antietam (or Sharpsburg) on September 17. Antietam was a battle Lee did not have to fight; after South Mountain, McClellan failed to pursue the retreating Confederates, and Lee could easily have slipped back across the Potomac.

Edward Porter Alexander, an artillerist in Lee's army, was blunt in calling it "the greatest military blunder that General Lee ever made." However, Alexander further observed that when McClellan brought his greatly superior army to the banks of Antietam Creek, "he brought himself also."

Lee was certain he could beat McClellan, and he gained a narrow tactical victory that day. Although it was the bloodiest single day in American military history, with total casualties of 22,717 dead, wounded and missing, Lee inflicted 20 percent more casualties than he suffered, despite being outnumbered two-to-one. Afterward, his army was too badly mauled to continue, and he had to retreat to Virginia. The profit of Sharpsburg was not worth the cost.

This is not to say that Lee was being overly aggressive in crossing the Potomac and marching north. With his army intact and rested and operating on ground of his own choosing, facing a general he was confident he could beat, Lee had every reason to believe he would win. In the fall of 1862, his troops and officers were in good form and good morale, and he was at the peak of his powers.

The conflict in Maryland forced Lee to surrender the strategic initiative for the first time since he had taken command, but thanks to the two generals who faced him next, this proved no disadvantage.

December saw McClellan's successor, Ambrose Burnside, hurl his army fruitlessly against the Army of Northern Virginia at Fredericksburg in perhaps the most senseless attack of the war. Longstreet remarked that as long as his ammunition held out and they kept coming, he would kill Yankee soldiers until there were none left in the North. As he watched a series of doomed Union soldiers run toward his line, Lee said, "It is well that war is so terrible - we should grow too fond of it."

The Battle of Fredericksburg was fought over four days beginning on December 11, 1862. Burnside had planned to cross the Rappahannock River and race to Richmond before Lee could stop him, but delays in setting up a pontoon bridge gave Lee time to move into position and ambush the Union forces with sharpshooters. The battle continued in the streets of Fredericksburg in the first major urban combat of the war and ended south of the city in defeat for the North. Casualties to the Union army totaled 12,653 while the Confederates lost 5,377 men. Reaction in the South was jubilant; the Richmond *Examiner* described it as a "stunning defeat to the invader, a splendid victory to the defender of the sacred soil."

Five months later, in May 1863, "Fighting Joe" Hooker challenged the Confederates. Lee again took advantage of the fact that his opponent was commanding an army in combat for the first time.

At Chancellorsville, Hooker faltered. "For once I lost confidence in Hooker," he admitted, "and that is all there is to it." Lee divided his forces in front of an army nearly twice the size of his own and sent Jackson on the flank attacks that had made his reputation. Jackson dispersed the Union forces, Lee moved forward, and Hooker hastily admitted defeat and retreated. This was Lee's "perfect battle."

But, for Lee and the Confederacy, the victory was marred by the news that Stonewall Jackson had died; with Jackson gone, Lee said, he had lost his right arm. His army had been reduced by more than 20 percent – with casualties totaling more than 13,000. The Confederacy, with its limited manpower, could not replace them. Some 17,000 Union soldiers had been lost, but these casualties comprised a smaller percentage of the 133,000-strong Union army.

Lee was confident that his army was virtually invincible. The Union was in shock; Lincoln, upon hearing news of the defeat, shouted, "My God! My God! What will the country say?" But Lee had one well-founded worry, first voiced when he heard that McClellan had been fired: "I fear they may continue to make these changes till they find someone whom I don't understand."

In opening the Gettysburg campaign a month after Chancellorsville, Lee was again challenging a Union general, George G. Meade, who was commanding an army in battle for the first time. Though it proved a victory for Meade, he wasn't the nemesis Lee had feared.

In the first two days of the fighting at Gettysburg, Lee nearly achieved the victory he and his comrades sought. First, two Confederate corps pushed the Union forces into the hills south of the town. But there, despite significant losses, the Union defenders held their position. Longstreet had received orders to attack, but got Lee's permission to wait for reinforcements.

Lee's blood was up, as Longstreet put it, and he continued the offensive without waiting for Longstreet's help. Determined to strike at the center of the Union line, Lee sent 12,500 men, under the command of three generals, across three-quarters of a mile of open field to high ground ominously called Cemetery Ridge. More than half of Lee's soldiers were killed in the attack.

Pickett's Charge - George Pickett was one of the generals who led the assault - marked the turning point in the war. "All this has been my fault - it is I that have lost the fight," Lee told Pickett's surviving soldiers. But as Lee retreated with his battered army, Meade – like McClellan – neglected to pursue and destroy him.

The two bruised armies sparred inconclusively through the autumn as the war's focus shifted west, where Vicksburg had fallen, giving the Union control of the Mississippi River, and Union forces threatened to break through Chattanooga to the Deep South. Longstreet's corps was sent west as reinforcement, and Davis proposed that Lee go there and take command. Lee said he would do so if the president wished, but he argued that the Western high command would never support a visiting general. And the question of who would command the Army of Northern Virginia remained open. Jackson was dead, Longstreet was in the West, and Lee could suggest no one else for the post. Davis agreed, and Lee remained in the East. In the weakening Confederacy, Lee's army was preeminent, and Lee was irreplaceable. But now Lincoln had put Ulysses S. Grant in charge of all his armies, and Lee's foreboding had materialized.

From a military perspective, Lee's contest against Grant in the spring and summer of 1864 was remarkable. With a steadily weakening army, and against a general who was at last a true match, Lee countered every advance, repelled every charge, and inflicted nearly twice the casualties his army suffered. At Petersburg, the two armies entered into a siege that lasted nine months. By the spring of 1865, Lee saw that final defeat was inevitable. "This is the people's war," he said. "When they tire, I stop."

In February, Lee had been appointed general in chief of all the Confederacy's armies, but by that point, there was little left for him to command. In line with his earlier call for the entire Southern nation to mobilize for war, he advocated arming slaves and freeing those who fought, saying, "I think we could at least do as well with them as the enemy." Slave owners resisted, but the first black units were in training as the war ended.

Lee attempted one last campaign, and he managed to extricate his army from Petersburg and bring it to the west, hoping to join Joe Johnston in North Carolina. But by the time he reached Appomattox Courthouse, he had only 8,000 armed men and knew he had to surrender.

General Porter Alexander urged Lee not to surrender but instead to let the men scatter to the hills to carry on a guerrilla war. Lee argued that such a strategy would mean ultimate ruin for the South; "a state of society would ensue from which it would take the country years to recover. . . . We have now simply to look the fact in the face that the Confederacy has failed."

6
ANTIETAM
– BRUCE CATTON

A whitewashed church without a steeple, a forty-acre field of corn that swayed in the autumn sun, an eroded country lane that rambled along a hillside behind a weathered snake-rail fence, and an arched stone bridge that crossed a lazy, copper-brown creek – this quiet Maryland landscape was the setting of one of the bloodiest days in American history - September 17, 1862.

Events had not gone in the Union's favor in the summer of 1862. The drive to capture Richmond, in which General George B. McClellan led the Army of the Potomac to the suburbs of the Confederate capital, had failed. In seven days, Robert E. Lee's outnumbered Rebels had driven McClellan's army to an uneasy refuge at Harrison's

Landing, a steaming mud flat far down the James River, miles from the goal which had been so nearly within reach.

A new Union army commanded by General John Pope had been sent to retrieve the situation. But Lee and his famous lieutenant, Stonewall Jackson, had shattered Pope's army so badly in the Second Battle of Bull Run, less than thirty miles from Washington, that Pope was sent to Minnesota to fight Indians for the rest of the war. Meanwhile, the remnants of his army crept back to Washington to be united with McClellan's Army of the Potomac. In the West, things were no better, with Confederates led by Braxton Bragg marching north into Kentucky.

As September began, the Union cause looked dark. The high hopes of spring - when people believed the war would be won in a month or so - had been replaced by bewilderment and discouragement. The most influential members of President Lincoln's Cabinet suspected that General McClellan might be a Southern sympathizer who did not want to win the war at all. The vital spark in the Northern war effort seemed to have died, and there did not appear to be a way to bring it back.

Lee's Army of Northern Virginia - ragged, weary, and worn, but imbued with the notion that there was no Yankee army anywhere it could not beat - had crossed the Potomac River and was aiming at nothing less than the conquest of Pennsylvania and the capture of Washington.

The Union also had to contend with the open threat of European intervention on the side of the Confederacy. From the beginning, the Confederates had depended on the British dependence on cotton, hoping to make the most of the South's exports to gain military support. Shipments to Europe ceased in the spring of 1861, with the implication that if the British wanted cotton, they should come get it. But England knew that siding with the South would put it at war with the United States, which would cut off wide-scale trade. The official British policy toward the American Civil War was neutrality, although many in the government were sympathetic to the South. It wouldn't take much to tip the Brits firmly into the Confederate camp.

In the fall of 1861, the United States Navy seized a British mail ship, the RMS *Trent*, with two Confederate diplomats aboard, suspected of carrying secret dispatches to London. The incident nearly sparked England's entry into the war. Eleven thousand British soldiers were sent to Canada, prepared to march on New York City if President Lincoln did not apologize and order the release of prisoners taken on the *Trent*. Lincoln relented, and crisis was averted. The following summer, U.S. and British relations were again strained by the discovery that a London shipbuilder had supplied the Confederacy with the warship CSS *Alabama*.

But the stakes were never higher than that September. The British considered the American war so far a stalemate. Lincoln's foreign minister in London, Charles Francis Adams – the son of former President John Quincy Adams and grandson of founding father John Adams – warned him that the British were preparing to step in to mediate the war. Adams believed that mediation could only benefit the South – that the British would recommend giving the Confederacy what it wanted: Independence. Mediation, however, hinged on General Lee's invasion of the North. If the Confederates were successful, the British leaders believed it would soften the Union's position, and make it more open to suggestion. Adams and Lincoln knew that any interference could only lead to war with England and that France – whose Emperor Napoleon III was reluctant to act without British collaboration – would not be far behind. The Union had only one way out: It had to win.

To revive the Northern war effort, Lincoln knew he must somehow bring into play the vigor and determination of the abolitionists. Thus far, official policy was that the war was being fought for the purpose of restoring the Union and that slavery had nothing to do with it. But Lincoln decided that if this could be made a war against slavery, as well as a war for reunion, no government would dare to intervene.

Lincoln had a draft of what would eventually be the Emancipation Proclamation, but Secretary of State William H. Seward had cautioned him that the timing had to be right. He argued that the proclamation could not be issued until the North had won a victory.

Lincoln restored McClellan to the poorly reorganized Army of the Potomac to try to defeat Lee in Maryland, despite the grumbling of Cabinet members and party leaders. Lincoln had been McClellan's most vocal critic, but he had to admit the general was a strong organizer and skilled trainer of troops, and it was in this capacity that the fractured Army of the Potomac needed him. "We must use what tools we have," Lincoln told his secretary John Hay.

Leaving two corps behind to defend Washington, McClellan marched six corps of about 84,000 men toward Maryland on September 5. Lee's Confederates were moving west of South Mountain, a long spur of the Blue Ridge that runs fifty miles northeast from the Potomac, cutting through western Maryland into Pennsylvania. The next week passed without incident, as each of the rivals tried to anticipate the other's move.

Screened by his cavalry, which held the South

Mountain passes with infantry support, Lee made a daring plan. McClellan, Lee knew, was slow; his march on Maryland was gaining six miles a day. Lee had two goals – to stop the Army of the Potomac at South Mountain, and capture the Union arsenal at Harpers Ferry – and decided he could accomplish both at once. He divided his army of about 45,000 into four sections, and sent three of those under the command of Stonewall Jackson to capture Harpers Ferry, which was defended by 12,000 Union soldiers. Lee gambled that his column of 18,000 men could hold the mountain until the rest could rejoin it.

There was one complication: Union soldiers discovered a copy of Lee's plans, wrapped around a package of cigars, in an abandoned Confederate camp. They delivered the document to McClellan on September 13. At noon, the general sent a telegram to Lincoln: "I have the whole rebel force in front of me, but I am confident, and no time shall be lost. I think Lee has made a gross mistake, and that he will be severely punished for it. I have all the plans of the rebels, and will catch them in their own trap if my men are equal to the emergency. . . . Will send you trophies."

The Union had the advantage; even half of the Army of the Potomac outnumbered Lee's entire force. McClellan could reinforce the post at Harpers Ferry and still send twice as many men against South Mountain as the force Lee had placed to defend it. But McClellan again was too cautious.

Instead of dispatching his troops immediately, McClellan gave orders for them to attack the next day. The delay allowed Stonewall Jackson to surround Harpers Ferry, get artillery into position to bombard it, and force its surrender before McClellan's reinforcements showed up. Lee was also tipped off by a Confederate sympathizer in McClellan's camp that his plans had been discovered and had time to adjust his strategy in the Maryland campaign.

The Confederates managed to hold back the Army of the Potomac for a day before couriers, galloping down the roads of western Maryland, arrived with Lee's orders to withdraw and reassemble at Sharpsburg, a little town just north of the Potomac. McClellan's men broke through the South Mountain passes, confident that the victory there had shifted the war's momentum in their favor. Whether the cause was confidence or caution is uncertain, but McClellan waited another day before attacking again. This gave Lee's exhausted army – the bulk of which had yet to return from Harpers Ferry - time to rest and regroup for the next bloody battle on the Antietam.

Lee put his men in position on the high ground just north of Sharpsburg on September 16, while McClellan's troops assembled on the hills opposite, on the far side of Antietam Creek. Lee's position was strong, but it had no depth. The Potomac River comes down from the north at Sharpsburg and then swings sharply to the east, with Sharpsburg lying inside the bend. Parallel to the big river and only a few miles east is Antietam Creek, with rolling high ground folded between creek and river. On this shallow thumb of land, the Yankees would have to come uphill to fight, but if the line broke anywhere, the entire Confederate army might be driven back to the river and destroyed.

Lee had two principal subordinates - the famous Jackson and the almost equally famous General James Longstreet, a tough fighter who was at his best on a defensive assignment. Jackson held the left - the high ground a mile or so north of Sharpsburg - with infantry massed in a big cornfield north of a little church and in a grove flanking the cornfield to the east. The center of the line, angling south and a little east from the church, was held by a division led by General D. H. Hill, under Longstreet's supervision; it occupied a sunken lane which zigzagged along near the crest of a rolling hill - a natural trench, as good as a fort. South of this position, on a hilltop just east of Sharpsburg, Longstreet had more men and artillery, with his extreme right posted to the south and east on some low hills overlooking the looping course of the Antietam.

McClellan ordered an attack at dawn on September 17. The first move was entrusted to McClellan's First Army Corps, led by "Fighting Joe" Hooker. A thin drizzle dimmed the early light as Hooker got his corps into line and began to move south along the road that ran from Sharpsburg toward Hagerstown, aiming for the church.

Hooker had three divisions in line - about 9,000 men. Preceded by skirmish lines, they approached the cornfield, found it full of armed Southerners, and wavered to a halt. On a ridge immediately behind the Union infantry, Hooker ordered up guns, and thirty-six of them, banked hub to hub, opened fire on the cornfield, plastering it unmercifully; cornstalks, knapsacks, muskets, and body parts flew in the air. When the bombardment stopped, the Union infantry moved in.

Through the cornfield and the woods just east of it, Hooker's divisions advanced, coming out on open ground facing the church. A counterattack by John B. Hood's division of Mississippi and Texas troops drove them back to their starting point. Reinforcements - the Federal 12th Corps under General Joseph K. F. Mansfield - regained the wood lot and the cornfield, driving out Hood's men and the remnants of the original Confederate line. Mansfield was killed, and Hooker was wounded. After two hours, and about 2,500 casualties, neither side had gained any ground. Hooker later wrote that the cornfield had been cut down by rifle and cannon fire as completely as if reapers had gone through with sickles, and Hood admitted that he was constantly worried that his horse would step on some wounded man.

McClellan sent in his Second Corps, led by Edwin Sumner. Sumner had three divisions of 5,000 to 6,000 men each, and he led one of these across the burnt-out cornfield into a woodland that flanked the church on the north and west, aiming to break the extreme left of the Confederate line. His advance was nearly unopposed at first - and then he ran into an ambush.

Portions of Lee's army were still coming in, finishing the cruel hike from Harpers Ferry, reaching him that morning in the nick of time. Lee sent them to Jackson's aid, and they hit Sumner's leading division in the flank, crumpling it with one savage blow and driving the division north in wild retreat, with heavy losses. For a moment, it looked as if the whole right of McClellan's army might be involved in the rout, but Hooker's huge line of guns on the ridge drove the triumphant Confederates back to the church. Across the cornfield - littered with at least 10,000 bodies from both armies - the rival forces glared at each other; although they continued to exchange rifle and artillery fire for the rest of the day, the real fighting in that part of the field was over.

Sumner brought up two more divisions to attack the Confederates in the sunken road. The Union divisions moved up to the deadly lane, were bombarded by Confederate fire, retreated, and reformed for another attack. The Confederate position was strong, but the Union advantage in numbers was great, and toward noon, one of Sumner's division commanders, General Israel B. Richardson, gained a hilltop where his infantry could enfilade the sunken roadway. The Confederates finally broke, and the Northerners swarmed in to claim the position. The lane was so heaped with dead and wounded men that soldiers on both sides referred to it as Bloody Lane.

Lee had lost the center of his position, and there were no reinforcements in sight. General D. H. Hill had picked up a musket and, with a handful of stragglers, was fighting like a foot soldier, while Longstreet was helping the gunners in a mangled battery. One assault would have broken Lee's line, and the Army of Northern Virginia might have been destroyed. But McClellan was worried. The men who had taken Bloody Lane were exhausted, General Richardson was mortally wounded, the entire right of his line was frazzled and unable to fight any more, and worst of all, he was holding in reserve the troops he might have sent in to exploit this success for fear Lee might mount a counterattack. A counterattack was the one thing Lee could not possibly manage; he could only hope that his men could stay where they were. But this never dawned on McClellan.

So the fighting died out along the center, just as it had farther north, and now the action shifted to the south. On the chain of low hills overlooking Antietam Creek, McClellan's 9th Corps, under General Ambrose E. Burnside, moved into action.

It moved ineptly, for Burnside threw his four divisions into action one at a time instead of massing them for a concerted attack. Although he had an advantage of four or five to one, he was never able to make it fully effective. He succeeded finally in storming the little stone bridge that led across the stream. He got one division across the creek a mile downstream - and after a long delay, in which ammunition was brought forward, and lines were rearranged, he sent his men to take the town of Sharpsburg, got between Lee and the Potomac, and made complete victory possible.

Lee had lost 10,000 men. The odds against his army were overwhelming.

Then, Confederate reinforcements arrived: A. P. Hill's division from Harpers Ferry, exhausted after a seventeen-mile hike. Hill, not a cautious man, drove his men unmercifully. Though he lost at least half of his division along the way, the ones who survived arrived at the exact moment they were needed, with Burnside's soldiers preparing to march on Sharpsburg and end the Southern Confederacy. Hill's soldiers came stamping up the hill from the Potomac and smote Burnside in the flank.

It was the push that settled things. The Yankees fell back. Burnside, as cautious as McClellan, conceived that he was in trouble and ordered his advance elements to withdraw. His advantage evaporated because he no longer thought it existed, and in a short time, he was sending frantic messages to McClellan announcing that he believed he could hold his position if heavily reinforced.

As a smoky dusk came down, the battle of Antietam came to an end.

The most amazing thing about this battle is that Lee held his army in position all through September 18, daring an opponent twice his size and with five times his reserves to come and fight him. McClellan did not; he held his forces together throughout the day, wondering if he might be attacked and hoping that he could hold his army in hand if that happened. On the night of September 18, Lee pulled his army out and went back across the Potomac to rest and recruit.

Even though he had played his hand with ruinous caution and had missed many opportunities, McClellan had won the decisive victory of the war. He won it, mostly, because he had not lost it - even though the fight was no better than a draw, Lee had to retreat. Because of this battle, Lee's dream of an invasion of the North came to nothing, England decided not to recognize the Confederacy, and the possibility that Europe would settle the American Civil War was forgotten. After Antietam, the Confederacy never again came within twenty-four hours of final victory; the Stars and Bars were on the downward slope, with great darkness at the end of the slide.

Antietam was a badly fought battle in the sense that it was miserably directed. The enlisted men paid for their generals' decisions. The casualty list of more than 22,000 killed and wounded for the two armies ranks it with the most dreadful battles ever waged by man. But this battle brought the country to and through a moment of enormous decision.

7
THE CIVIL WAR'S GREATEST SCOOP
– JAMES WEEKS

New York throbbed with the usual breakfast-hour bustle on September 19, 1862, apparently undisturbed by the recent Confederate invasion of Northern soil. But when a crowd of newsboys burst from Park Row's *Tribune* building, barking "Extra!" the response revealed the tension on the streets. Weary of newspaper rumors about a great battle in Maryland, New Yorkers crowded about the newsboys, hoping for some real information. They got it. Here were no vague claims of "Great and Glorious Victory" or "Great Slaughter of the Rebels." Instead, the *Tribune* offered six columns of accurate, forceful prose about the Battle of Antietam, fought two days before.

The same paper that only the previous morning had been forced to admit that "our latest intelligence from the seat of war . . . is little else than mere rumor" now boasted the first complete account of Antietam. Far more than a scoop, the article was a masterpiece of battle reporting. It took readers on a tour of the terrain; graphically depicted the assaults of Generals Joseph Hooker, Edwin Sumner, and Ambrose Burnside, and impartially assessed the struggle's tactics and results. All this in 7,000 words, and in the hands of the public less than thirty-six hours after the conflict.

The author's identity was as mysterious as the story's appearance that Friday morning. No byline accompanied the story when it was reprinted in 1,200 newspapers across the North. Even when the *Tribune* published a laudatory editorial about its "Special Correspondent," it omitted the reporter's name. The *Tribune* revealed that "the writer . . . had a portion of his coat torn from his shoulders by a fragment of shell, and the horse he rode carried off from the field two Rebel bullets in his body."

We now know the writer was George Washburn Smalley, who worked as a correspondent during the Maryland campaign. Smalley would go on to become the foremost foreign correspondent of his day.

Smalley was born on June 2, 1833, in Franklin, Massachusetts – son of a Congregational minister and prominent lawyer, and a direct descendant of Pilgrims. He was an ivy-league-educated barrister – with degrees from Yale University and Harvard Law School – and spoke with a pronounced Boston accent. He married abolitionist Wendell Phillips's daughter.

Upon passing the bar, Smalley had joined his father's law firm. In 1858, he branched out on his own, borrowing money to start his own practice in Boston. When he failed to obtain a loan to cover rising debts in mid-1861, his influential future father-in-law wrote a letter to Sydney Howard Gay, a *Tribune* editor, recommending Smalley for a correspondent's job. The letter kicked off the career of perhaps the greatest newspaperman of the Victorian era.

The *Tribune's* editor, Horace Greeley, an acquaintance of Smalley's father, promised the fledgling reporter great adventure. Greeley, the son of poor farmers from New Hampshire, first became fascinated with the power of the press at age fifteen, as a printer's apprentice to Amos Bliss, editor of the East Poultney, Vermont, newspaper *Northern Spectator*.

Greeley moved to New York City in 1831, set up his own print shop, and in 1833 published his first daily newspaper, the *New York Morning Post,* which was a financial failure. With profits from his 80,000-circulation Whig Party periodical

Log Cabin, Greeley founded the *Tribune* in 1841. Its first issue, on April 10 of that year, sold 5,000 copies at a penny apiece; it featured coverage of a memorial parade in New York for President William Henry Harrison, who had died the week before from pneumonia. Over the next two decades, the *Tribune's* readership grew to 200,000, making it the most-circulated daily newspaper in the United States.

Greeley, fifty years old in 1861, was determined that the *Tribune* would cover the Civil War as no war had been covered before. Northern newspapers sent about 150 correspondents onto the battlefields; more than half of those were employed by the *Tribune* and the *Herald.* At the start of the war, the *Tribune* coined the phrase "On to Richmond" to urge Union occupation of the Confederate capital in Virginia. The *Tribune* had an abolitionist slant, which suited Smalley. In an impassioned editorial on August 20, 1862, Greeley pressed Lincoln to free slaves. Headlined "Prayer of Twenty Millions," the editorial elicited a famous reply from Lincoln: "My paramount object in this struggle *is* to save the Union, and is *not* either to save or to destroy slavery."

In early 1862, Smalley was assigned to cover Major General John C. Frémont's futile Shenandoah Valley campaign. At the Battle of Cross Keys, he displayed his journalistic precocity by soundly scooping rival New York correspondents with his account of Frémont's defeat at the hands of Confederate General Stonewall Jackson. In June 1862, Smalley shifted his beat when Frémont's command merged with the newly formed Army of Virginia, which suffered a bitter defeat in August under General John Pope at Second Bull Run.

The War Department had issued an order banning correspondents from the Army, and Pope's successor, the reinstated George McClellan, loathed them. But Smalley's acquaintance, General "Uncle" John Sedgwick, offered him a position as a volunteer aide-de-camp. Smalley quickly found a captain's uniform and joined the Army of the Potomac in early September as it shadowed the triumphant Army of Northern Virginia's northward incursion onto Union soil.

It all happened a bit too quickly for Smalley. Expecting to camp out for just one night, he packed only a raincoat and a toothbrush. He was gone six weeks.

Smalley discovered he enjoyed trotting along with the blue columns through the early fall haze. The Army of the Potomac fought through the South Mountain passes on September 14 in an attempt to destroy the Rebel army piecemeal. Smalley watched as the blue waves progressed up the mountain terrain against weak but stubborn Confederate resistance.

Another writer shared Smalley's vantage point at the back of the Union pack. Albert D. Richardson was also employed by the *Tribune*, though he and Smalley had never met. In casual conversation, the two were astonished to discover they both had been born in Franklin, Massachusetts, in 1833. But there was little time to talk as Smalley and Richardson parted to cover the battle from different perspectives.

Smalley risked revealing his identity by sidling in next to General McClellan and his staff. At close range, Smalley thought "an air of indecision hung about" the commander once called a "young Napoleon." He later wrote: "There was in his appearance something prepossessing if not commanding: something rather scholarly than warlike; amiable, well-bred, cold, and yet almost sympathetic. His troops were slowly forcing their way up the steep mountain side upon which we looked. It was, in fact, from a military point of view, a very critical moment, but this general commanding had a singular air of detachment; almost that of a disinterested spectator: or of a general watching manoeuvres. . . . There he stood, an interesting figure; as if star-gazing. Compact, square-chested, his face well-molded."

After the Union troops had dislodged the gray defenders late on September 14, the newspaperman accompanied the subsequent march to Sharpsburg,

Maryland, site of what would become the Battle of Antietam. There, Smalley reported, McClellan "in his usual accommodating spirit" wasted two precious days without launching an attack, allowing Robert E. Lee to collect his scattered forces.

On the afternoon of September 16, Smalley and Richardson visited Major General Joseph Hooker's headquarters on the Union right, where they were told that "Fighting Joe's" Corps would deliver the initial Union punch. Because neither reporter knew Hooker or any of his staff, Smalley thought it odd that their presence was ignored completely by the entourage: "For aught they knew I might have been a Rebel spy."

Smalley and Richardson tagged along as General Hooker followed a cavalry contingent he had ordered to probe the Rebel left. When artillery fire signaled that the Union cavalry had brushed the Confederate lines, Smalley and Richardson spurred ahead to watch the action. Dozens of blue troopers galloped back to the safety of the Union lines, and shot and shell showered around Hooker and his staff. Smalley later described Hooker's eyes gleaming "with the fierce joy of battle" as the general drove forward with his infantry. He "played the game of war as the youngest member of a football team plays football," Smalley wrote. "He had to the full that joy of battle which McClellan never had at all; and showed it."

With nightfall approaching, Hooker decided to break off the action. "If they had let us start earlier, we might have finished tonight," Smalley heard the general mutter. "Tomorrow we fight the battle that will decide the fate of the Republic." Like the Union boys who slept on their guns that restless night, Smalley curled up under the stars with his horse's bridle wrapped around one arm.

As Hooker's corps bowled into the Confederate forces at dawn, Smalley was off in pursuit of the general, whom he found in an exposed position. With his staff sent away on assignments, Hooker beckoned Smalley and asked him to carry an order. "Tell the colonel of that regiment to take his men to the front and keep them there," Hooker said, gesturing toward Union soldiers falling back from a Rebel onslaught.

Smalley obliged, but when he delivered the order, the regimental commander refused to accept it. "Very good," Smalley snapped back. "I will report to General Hooker that you decline to obey."

"For God's sake, don't do that!" the colonel cried. "The Rebels are too many for us, but I had rather face them than Hooker."

Returning to Hooker, Smalley was instructed not to "let the next man talk so much" and was sent off again. "Order every regiment you can find to advance," Hooker shouted. "It is time to end this business." Smalley found Hooker in the thick of combat when he finished his assignments; soon after, the general went down with a wound – shot through the foot by a Confederate sharpshooter while astride his conspicuous white horse. Smalley was disappointed that his new acquaintance had to retire from the field.

Antietam was characterized by desperate but uncoordinated attacks by Union forces, as well as McClellan's hesitancy to seize opportunities. As Smalley trotted near McClellan's headquarters in the afternoon, he was hailed by Lieutenant James Harrison Wilson of the commander's staff. Wilson, who knew Smalley had been with Hooker earlier in the day, asked him to see if the wounded general could take command of the Army of the Potomac. "Most of us think that this battle is only half fought and half won," Wilson said. "There is still time to finish it. But McClellan will do no more." Smalley demurred, warning Wilson that what he suggested was an act of mutiny. "I know that as well as you do," Wilson replied, but it was "the only way to crush Lee and end the rebellion and save the country." Smalley told the lieutenant to forget it, that the bearer of the message probably would face arrest and worse. Wilson backed down, asking Smalley simply to prod Hooker back to the field. The writer reluctantly accepted this new mission.

He found Hooker in bed, his usual ruddy complexion white with pain. Smalley spoke broadly about the day's indecisive combat, causing Hooker to explode with "language of extreme plainness" against McClellan's "excessive caution and systematic inertness." Smalley took a more direct approach, asking Hooker if he might return to command his corps some other way - in a carriage perhaps. "It is impossible," Hooker answered. "I cannot move. I am perfectly helpless." He grilled Smalley about the motivation behind his question, believing someone must have put the writer up to it. Smalley explained that some of the general's friends were curious about his ability to resume command in case of an emergency. "You see what a wreck I am," Hooker said in agony. "It is impossible." Smalley left.

Smalley's departure from Hooker's bedside ended the relationship that had developed between general and reporter, but the admiration of each man for the other lingered. In his account of the battle, Smalley praised Hooker's "bravery and soldierly ability," while Hooker later said of Smalley, "In all the experience which I have had of war, I never saw the most experienced and veteran soldier exhibit more tranquil fortitude and unshaken valor than was exhibited by that young man." In fact, Hooker later tapped Smalley for staff service when the general was elevated to command the Army of the Potomac.

As nightfall brought an end to the slaughter of September 17, Smalley and his three *Tribune* colleagues met to compare notes in a farmhouse jammed with wounded. Smalley, whose misgivings about McClellan told him the battle would not be renewed the following day, agreed to somehow dispatch an account of the day's action to New York. After pilfering some Army grub and trading his mount for a fresher one, Smalley was in the saddle by 9:00 p.m., headed for Frederick, Maryland, the only town in the vicinity that might have accessible telegraph service. Having dozed in the saddle for most of the thirty-mile journey, Smalley trotted into Frederick early in the morning of September 18. The telegraph office was closed, and Smalley huddled up near the doorway to nap.

The telegraph operator who appeared at 7:00 a.m. could not promise Smalley his account would go through to New York because the telegraph wires had been commandeered by the War Department for military use. Smalley seated himself and began writing: "The greatest battle of the war was fought to-day, lasting from daylight till dark, and closing without decisive result." He handed his scribbled manuscript to the operator sheet by sheet until a full newspaper column had been tapped out.

As the telegrapher had predicted, the story was relayed directly to the War Department in Washington, where it became the first news

Secretary Edwin M. Stanton had of Antietam, with the exception of McClellan's brief dispatch announcing victory. Stanton passed the story on to President Lincoln, who had it read to his Cabinet. That night, the *Tribune*'s Washington correspondent wrote that "all that is really known about the battle here is derived from that dispatch." Finally, it was released to New York and appeared in the *Tribune*'s Friday, September 19, edition.

Smalley hoped to draft a longer account of the battle but hesitated to wire any more news from Frederick. He decided to jump an eastbound train and telegraph the story from Baltimore, and he got there just ten minutes before the New York express was scheduled to leave for Washington. Smalley faced a crucial decision: Should he wire the story from Baltimore or deliver it to the *Tribune* in person? He hopped aboard the New York express.

Smalley's coach was lit by a single flickering oil lamp at the end of the car. Sitting, he could barely see at all, but by standing next to the lamp, he had enough light to write. With the stub of a pencil, he began scribbling, beginning his account with a powerful lead: "Fierce and desperate battle between 200,000 men has raged since daylight, yet night closes on an uncertain field. It is the greatest fight since Waterloo - all over the field contested with an obstinacy equal even to Waterloo."

Since he had spent the morning of the battle on

the Union left, his account of the savage fighting in the cornfield made particularly provocative copy: "Forward, was the word, and on went the line with a cheer and a rush. Back across the corn-field, leaving dead and wounded behind them, over the fence, and across the road, and then back again into the dark woods which closed around them, went the retreating Rebels.

> Meade and his Pennsylvanians followed hard and fast . . . . But out of those gloomy woods came suddenly and heavily terrible volleys - volleys which smote, and bent, and broke in a moment that eager front . . . . In ten minutes the fortune of the day seemed to have changed - it was the Rebels now who were advancing, pouring out of the woods in endless lines, sweeping through the corn field from which their comrades had just fled. . . .

> Every hill-top, ridge and woods along the whole line was crested and veiled with white clouds of smoke. All day had been clear and bright since the early cloudy morning, and now this whole magnificent, unequaled scene shone with the splendor of an afternoon September sun. Four miles of battle, its glory all visible, its horrors all veiled, the fate of the Republic hanging on the hour - could any one be insensible of its grandeur. . . .

Smalley did not spare his readers the cost of that panoply: "The field and its ghastly harvest which the reaper had gathered in those fatal hours remained finally with us . . . . The dead are strewn so thickly that as you ride over it you cannot guide your horse's steps too carefully. Pale and bloody faces are everywhere upturned. They are sad and terrible, but there is nothing which makes one's heart beat so quickly as the imploring look of sorely wounded men who beckon wearily for help which you cannot stay to give."

The writer paused in Jersey City to switch from train to the dawn ferry to New York; by the time it docked, he had composed 7,000 words on Antietam. More than a chronology of events, this report offered astute insight into the failure of McClellan's battle plan: "It is impossible not to suppose that the attacks on right and left were meant in a measure to correspond, for otherwise the enemy had only to repel Hooker on the one hand, then transfer his troops, and hurl them against Burnside. . . . Still more unfortunate in its results was the total failure of these separate attacks on the right and left to sustain, or in any manner co-operate with each other."

Smalley rushed the scrawled pages to the *Tribune*. Gay had been notified in advance that an important dispatch was expected, so when Smalley stumbled into the office, it was crowded with waiting compositors and printers. At 6:00 a.m., the crew began typesetting the nearly illegible manuscript. Two hours later, the six-column story of Antietam hit the streets.

Smalley's story came to be regarded as the best account of a Civil War battle.

8
BELLE BOYD, CONFEDERATE SPY
– RICHARD F. SNOW

S he began her career as a spy and ended it as an actress – professions layered with myth and lies. One historian concluded she had never lived at all. But Belle Boyd was, in the words of Douglas Southall Freeman, "one of the most active and most reliable of the many secret woman agents of the Confederacy."

Boyd was born in Martinsburg, Virginia, on May 9, 1844, to Mary Rebecca and Benjamin Reed Boyd, a prosperous store owner. She described her childhood as the idyllic, care-free life of a tomboy who climbed trees and raced through the woods with her brothers, sisters, and cousins. Her hometown – nestled in the Shenandoah Valley – was populated by some of the most respectable families of "The Old Dominion": the descendants of Thomas Fairfax, a British lord who financed early settlement of the Virginia colony, and the Warringtons, whom novelist William Makepeace Thackeray immortalized in his novel, *The Virginians*. Martinsburg was also a town on the rise, its importance buoyed by the engine and machine shops of the Baltimore and Ohio Railroad that were erected in the late 1840s.

But Belle was most impressed by the town's natural beauty. "Imagine a bright warm sun shining upon a pretty two-storied house," she wrote of her childhood home, "the walls of which are completely hidden by roses and honeysuckle in most luxuriant bloom. At a short distance in front of it flows a broad, clear, rapid stream: around it the silver maples wave their graceful branches in the perfume-laden air of the South."

When she was twelve, Boyd was sent to Baltimore, Maryland, to study French, music, and the classics at Mount Washington Female College. When she turned sixteen, she was introduced into Washington society. The year was 1860; within a few months, the country would be divided by Civil War. But that spring, for Boyd, was filled "with all the high hopes and thoughtless joy natural to my time of life." She didn't dream, she wrote, "how soon my youth was to be blasted with a curse."

Boyd attended theaters "crowded to excess." She

listened as great and statesmen gave speeches in the halls of Congress. "... for the last time for many years to come," she remembered, "the daughters of the North and South commingled in sisterly love and friendship. . . . we ate and drank, we dined and danced . . . without a thought of the volcano that was seething beneath our feet."

The ripples of rebellion were unmistakable that winter, with the election of President Abraham Lincoln decided. Boyd soon was at odds with her society friends from the North. When Virginia voted to secede from the Union the following April, Boyd returned home to Martinsburg, excited about contributing to the cause. Recruits were being rallied for the Confederate army, and Boyd's father Benjamin was one of the first to volunteer. Because of his social stature, Benjamin was offered a commission as an officer, but elected to leave the post open for someone else who might benefit more from the pay. He was assigned to the ranks of the 2nd Virginian – a regiment commanded by General Thomas J. Jackson, who had not yet earned his famous nickname "Stonewall;" the unit would later be known as the "Stonewall Brigade." Boyd joined with other women to raise money to arm and equip her father's regiment, whose colors included the inscription: "Our God, our country, and our women."

The 2nd Virginian was called to defend the arsenal

at Harpers Ferry on April 27, 1861, and the absence of the men cast a pall over Martinsburg. "My home had now become desolate and lonely," Boyd wrote, ". . . and the reaction of feeling had set in." The effects of depression were most pronounced in her mother, Mary, whose face wore "an anxious, careworn expression." Mary, the daughter of an old officer and orphaned very young, had been sixteen when she married Benjamin Boyd; now she was separated from him for the first time.

Boyd tried to distract herself with books, and with assembling packets of provisions to be sent to her father in the field. But, she wrote, "I soon found these employments too tame and monotonous to satisfy my temperament, and I made up my mind to pay a visit to the camp."

The arsenal at Harpers Ferry had been in ruins when Jackson's brigades arrived, stripped of weapons and burned by a Union general named Roger Jones so it could not aid the Confederates. But Jackson had been able to salvage machines, tools, and rifle stocks, which he had shipped to Richmond, and set to fortifying the town. Boyd encountered "an animated scene," at Harpers Ferry with "officers and men as gay and joyous as though no bloody strife awaited them." But that was to be short-lived. Amid rumors that 5,000 Union soldiers were marching toward the camp, Boyd said goodbye to her father and returned home.

She was awakened by the distant roar of artillery at 5:00 a.m. on July 3, 1861. Jackson's troops were fighting an advance Union guard about eight miles from Martinsburg, in a spot called Falling Waters. Five hours later, the Stonewall Brigades marched through town in retreat. Two Southern soldiers, injured in the fight, were left at the Martinsburg hospital, where they were the only patients.

Boyd was at the hospital bedside of one of the injured soldiers, who was "ranting in a violent fit of delirium," when she heard heavy footsteps. She turned to face an infantry captain and two soldiers, carrying a Union flag which they waved over the wounded rebels. "Sir," Boyd said, "these men are as helpless as babies, and have, as you may see, no power to reply to your insults."

The next day, Independence Day, Union soldiers "inflamed by drink and hatred," according to Boyd, began looting houses. At the Boyd home, they produced "a large Federal flag, which they were now preparing to hoist over our roof in token of our submission to their authority." Boyd's mother stepped forward and said, "Every member of my household will die before that flag shall be raised over us." When one of the soldiers replied in "language as offensive as it is possible to conceive," Boyd shot him dead.

Fearing the soldiers were plotting to burn their home with them in it, Boyd sent a message to the Union commander, who put a stop to it. The commander investigated the shooting and determined that Boyd had "done perfectly right." He seemed to admire her pluck.

Not only did Boyd go unpunished for killing a Union soldier, she was protected. The commander placed sentries around her home, and Union officers regularly checked to make sure the occupants had no complaints. One of the officers gave Boyd a pistol – "a token, he was pleased to say, of his admiration of the spirit I had shown in defence of my mother and my home."

The officers grew comfortable with Boyd. She was often within earshot of conversations that disclosed Union positions and plans. "It was in this way that I became acquainted with so many of them," Boyd wrote in her memoirs, "an acquaintance 'the rebel spy' did not fail to turn to account on more than one occasion." She committed all she heard to memory, and later, to paper. Through trusted messengers, she began to funnel the intelligence to nearby Confederate camps. The first of these notes were passed to Lieutenant Colonel James Ewell Brown "Jeb" Stuart, who commanded an infantry regiment in the Shenandoah Valley. "Through accident or by treachery," Boyd wrote, "one of these missives fell into the Yankees' hands." Enthusiastic and inexperienced, she had made no effort at cipher or to disguise her handwriting, and was easily identified as the culprit.

Given the opportunity to deny her involvement, Boyd instead confessed. According to the Articles of War, she was told, the penalty for giving food, ammunition, information or aid to abet the enemies of the United States Government was death, "or whatever penalty the honourable members of the Court-martial shall see fit to inflict." Despite the threat, she was released with only a reprimand and the promise that she would be watched closely. Boyd was undaunted; "my little rebel heart was on fire," she wrote, "and I indulged in thoughts and plans of vengeance."

Boyd resumed her spy work. She not only passed information to the Confederates but also, whenever possible, pistols and swords that she stole from Union soldiers and concealed in her clothes. These she sent to General Jackson's brigades – still equipping her father's regiment, only now with the weapons of his enemy. One of Boyd's messengers was a friend about her own age, who in her memoirs she called "Miss Sophia B." Sophia, who had brothers in the 2nd Virginian, once walked seven miles to deliver a letter to General Jackson.

On July 17, Union soldiers left Martinsburg for Charles Town, and the town was reclaimed by the Confederates. Boyd's hometown would change hands thirty-seven times over the course of the war.

A week later, Boyd was visiting an aunt and uncle just south of Winchester in Front Royal when an order arrived from the Confederate command that the hospital there was to be prepared for injured soldiers from Manassas. The Confederates had just won the First Battle of Bull Run – a victory that earned General Jackson his nickname. "There stands Jackson like a stone wall!" a soldier yelled. "Rally behind the Virginians!" But more than 1,500 Rebels had been wounded.

Boyd helped to lead the hospital effort and was installed as one of the matrons. She was still only seventeen. The next six to eight weeks were exhausting, as the "suffering heroes" poured in from the field. Boyd was relieved that her father was not among them. But the incessant nursing took its toll on her health, and she returned to her home in Martinsburg to rest.

In October, Boyd and her mother resolved to pay a short visit to her father's camp at Manassas, nearly seventy miles east. They stayed at a large house in the center of the camp, and the Confederate leaders quickly put Boyd to work. She often acted as a courier between Generals Jackson and P. G. T. Beauregard, on whom most of the credit for the victory at Bull Run had been bestowed.

After a few weeks, the Boyd women returned to Martinsburg for an uneventful winter. Boyd's father, on sick leave, joined them there for much of

February 1862. Ready to rejoin his regiment, Boyd was aware of Union forces approaching the town. He sent his daughter to Front Royal. By March 3, Martinsburg was again under Union control.

Trouble followed Boyd to Front Royal. On March 23, Stonewall Jackson's army clashed with a Union infantry division commanded by Colonel Nathan Kimball at Kernstown, less than twenty miles north. Jackson led the charge in hopes of weakening the Unions' hold on the Shenandoah Valley, but he underestimated Kimball and was dealt a rare defeat. With the Confederates in retreat and the Union army descending on Front Royal, Boyd's aunt and uncle fled for Richmond. Boyd decided she would be safer with her mother in Martinsburg. She set out with her maid. They made it as far as the train station in Winchester, where Boyd was recognized and arrested by a Union officer who was transporting Confederate prisoners to Baltimore.

Boyd worked her charms on her captors. On the train to Baltimore, she recognized and sat next to a man who was afraid of being discovered with a small Confederate flag he concealed in his pocket. Boyd took it from him and laughing, raised it over their heads. "The first emotions of the Union officer and his men were those of indignation," she wrote, "but better feelings succeeded, and they allowed it was an excellent joke that a convoy of Confederate prisoners should be brought in under a Confederate flag, and that flag raised by a lady." She was confined at Eutaw House, one of Baltimore's best hotels, but granted visits by her Southern friends. After a week, Boyd was sent home to Martinsburg.

Though no longer a prisoner, Boyd was watched closely, and her movements limited. "All the mischief done to the Federal cause was laid at my charge," she remembered, "and it is with unfeigned joy and true pride I confess that the suspicions of the enemy were far from being unfounded." Boyd's mother sought and was granted permission for the two of them to join family members in Richmond. They would stop first in Front Royal, the scene of Boyd's most famous exploit.

Boyd arrived to find her aunt's house commandeered as a Union headquarters. She and her mother were allowed to rest in a small cottage on the grounds. But Boyd made her way into the residence, where she met Union officers who were preparing for a war council. The officers told Boyd General Jackson was about to be "whipped." As the council assembled in the home's drawing room, Boyd snuck into an upstairs bedroom. She found a hole that had been bored through the floor and put her ear to it. She listened for hours as the council made its plans.

On May 23, Jackson, moving north on the

offensive that would bring him to the Potomac, was preparing to attack Front Royal. The Union forces, falling back from the town, planned to burn the bridges behind them.

Boyd "did not stop to reflect . . . [but] started at a run down the street, which was thronged with Union officers and men," she recounted in her memoirs. "I soon cleared the town and gained the open fields . . . hoping to escape observation until such time as I could make my way to the Confederate line. . . . I had on a dark-blue dress, with a little fancy white apron over it, and this contrast of colors, being visible at a great distance, made me far more conspicuous than was just then agreeable." Union pickets opened fire, and "the rifle-balls flew thick and fast about me," she wrote, "and more than one struck the ground so near my feet as to throw the dust in my eyes."

She reached the Rebel lines and delivered her message. Jackson drove the Yankees back, took the bridges, and then wrote Boyd a note: "I thank you, for myself and for the army, for the immense service that you have rendered your country to-day."

Boyd helped prepare a hospital at her aunt's home for the wounded Confederate. Under close watch again, Boyd was surprised by the appearance in her aunt's drawing-room of two men dressed in Confederate uniforms. They told her they had been pardoned and given passes to return to their homes. Boyd's maid thought she recognized one of the men and warned her that he was a Union spy. Boyd ignored the warning and gave one of the men a letter to pass to Jackson. The maid was right; Boyd's letter was delivered instead to a Union general. Boyd was arrested, and Secretary of War Edwin M. Stanton drafted the order that had her jailed in Washington.

Before being escorted from Front Royal, Boyd was forced to submit to a search of the home and belongings. Her maid rushed to the kitchen to burn some incriminating documents, but others were discovered in Boyd's writing desk and confiscated, along with the pistol. A cavalry unit of 450 men escorted her out of the South.

The journey was exhausting; Boyd convinced her escort to pause for a few hours at her Martinsburg home. But these men were not so sympathetic. They ignored the pleas of Boyd's mother to leave her and forget their mission. Ransacking the home in search of more evidence, they came up empty and pushed on to Washington. "My nearest and dearest were lamenting around me," Boyd wrote, "and within minutes I was to be torn from their arms and consigned to the doubtful mercies of strangers and enemies."

In Washington, a *New York Tribune* reporter saw Boyd wearing "a gold palmetto tree beneath her beautiful chin, a Rebel soldier's belt around her waist, and a velvet band across her forehead, with the seven stars of the Confederacy shedding their pale light therefrom." The *New York Herald's* correspondent was less dazzled; he dismissed her as "an accomplished prostitute."

Her confinement was not in a cozy cottage or fine hotel, but the Old Capitol Prison, "a vast brick building, like all prisons, somber, chilling, and repulsive." From the window of her cell, Boyd could glimpse the homes on Pennsylvania Avenue where she had made her debut into society. "I could not help indulging in reminiscences of my last visit to Washington," she wrote, "and contrasting it with my present forlorn condition."

But Boyd's hardship was a good deal less severe than the typical prisoner's. She was given special considerations; some believed the prison's superintendent had fallen in love with her. Though Stanton had ordered a bread-and-water diet for her, she was regularly served soup, steak, chicken, corn, tomatoes, Irish stew, potatoes, and fresh fruit. A servant brought her tea and newspapers each evening. As long as she behaved, her cell door was left open. After a month came the unexpected news that she was being released.

Boyd was part of a prisoner exchange that sent 200 back to the South early in 1863. She was put on a boat for Richmond, where she was welcomed by her aunt. Later, she was reclaimed by her father, who took her home to Martinsburg, which was once again in the hands of the Confederates. Stonewall Jackson, upon seeing Boyd, patted her head and said, "God bless you, my child." The general pledged to keep her safe, by keeping her informed of his army's movements. He sent Boyd to Winchester and commissioned her as his honorary aide-de-camp. She spent some time in Charlottesville and, after Union forces again seized Martinsburg, fled Virginia for Knoxville, Tennessee, on Jackson's orders. In May 1863, her tour of the South took her to Mobile, Alabama, where she received sad news.

There was a rumor that Jackson had been wounded at the Battle of Chancellorsville. A telegraph confirmed her fears: The general had died, and "now lies in state at the Governor's mansion." Devastated, Boyd wore a black band on her left arm; "the sorrow of the South is unmitigated and inextinguishable," she wrote later. She made her way back to Martinsburg. Soon after, her hometown "became one vast hospital," as wounded Confederates were sent back South from the devastating battle at Gettysburg, Pennsylvania.

Within days, the Union army had reclaimed Martinsburg, and Boyd was arrested again. She was jailed in Washington's Carroll Prison, a large brick building that had formerly been a hotel. She had the best cell available, but over the next five months, she contracted typhoid fever. Her father traveled to Washington and pleaded for Boyd's sentence to be commuted. The request was granted, with one condition: Boyd was banished to the South, never again to return to the North. When Boyd reached Richmond in December 1863, she learned that her father had died.

Boyd longed to get away; to return to good health, she told Confederate President Jefferson Davis; she wanted to travel to Europe. Davis gave Boyd her final mission: She was to act as courier, delivering messages to Confederate sympathizers in Great Britain. On May 8, 1864, she boarded a ship in Wilmington. The ship, called the *Greyhound*, sailed under a British flag, and its passengers included Edward A. Pollard, editor of the *Richmond Examiner*. Before it was out of sight of the American coastline, the *Greyhound* was spotted and pursued by a Union steamship. The sea echoed with cannon fire, until the captain of the *Greyhound* announced, "We must surrender!" Boyd destroyed the dispatches she was carrying to England, rather than have them fall into Union hands. Her mission was over.

Her charm apparently survived; Samuel Wylde Hardinge, the Union officer who took command of her captured ship, promptly asked her to marry him. The attraction was mutual. "His every movement," she said, "was so much that of a refined gentleman that my 'Southern proclivities,' strong as they were, yielded . . . to the impulses of my heart."

After diverting the *Greyhound* to Boston, where its passengers and crew were arrested, Hardinge went to Washington to plead for Boyd's release. She was escorted to Canada, and warned that if she was caught again in the United States, she would be shot. She boarded another ship for London, where she rendezvoused with Hardinge and married him. He died shortly after the war, however, leaving her penniless in England with an infant daughter. When her memoirs brought in less income than she had hoped, she turned to the stage in 1866, opening in Manchester in a romantic comedy by Edward Bulwer-Lytton. She had an immense success, which continued when she returned to America.

She married again - this time to an English military man - but it was not a happy match. "My health was failing," she said years later in a brief, pathetic statement, "and I went with my husband to California. Just previous to the birth of my little son my mind gave way and my child was born in the asylum for the insane at Stockton, Cal. My boy was buried there."

Her eventual recovery and the birth of two more daughters did not reconcile her to her husband. She divorced him in 1884 and, less than six weeks later, married Nat High, an actor seventeen years her junior. She returned to the stage, but was forced to play second-class houses. The war had been over for twenty years, and people were no longer so intrigued by the glamorous spy.

On Sunday, June 10, 1900, she wrote her daughters from Evansville, Wisconsin, where she planned to give a recitation for the local Civil War veterans in the Grand Army of the Republic: "I feel like a criminal not sending you money. But I have only been able to play one night, and sent you all I had . . . over expenses, 2.00."

The next morning, she had a heart attack and died. The women's auxiliary of the G.A.R. raised the money for her funeral, and four Union veterans lowered her coffin into Northern soil. Carved into her gravestone, "erected by a comrade," was the identity she bore with pride: "Confederate spy . . . born in Virginia."

9
THE MIRACLE THAT
SAVED THE UNION
– SCARRITT ADAMS

To save the Union fleet, something special was needed to confront the ironclad warship the Confederacy was building. Yet it took a visit from President Lincoln to the somnolent offices of the Navy Department to force the issue, and by then, it was so late that the Navy had to have a miracle. The contractor would have to design and build, in just 100 days, a ship whose like had never been seen.

To build its miracle ship, the Navy required a miracle man: inventor John Ericsson. Born in 1803 in Sweden to a speculator and mine supervisor, Ericsson and his older brother Nils were child prodigies. In 1810, while their father was directing the excavation of the Swedish Göta

Canal, the brothers became apprentices to that project's architect, Baltzar von Platen. By the age of fourteen, Ericsson was working as a surveyor; his assistant carried a footstool that he needed to reach his instruments. He joined the Swedish army at seventeen, and quickly rose to the rank of lieutenant. While surveying for the army in northern Sweden, Ericsson dabbled in mechanical engineering, building in his spare time an engine that ran on heat rather than steam.

In 1826, Ericsson resigned from the Swedish army to pursue engineering in England. Three years later, with partner John Braithwaite, he built a steam locomotive prototype called the *Novelty*, which he entered in the Rainhill Trials, competing with four other inventors for a contract with the Liverpool and Manchester Railway. While Ericsson's engine was the fastest of the five, it lost because of persistent boiler problems. Two more locomotive designs failed to find a buyer, and Ericsson spent most of 1832 in debtors' prison.

The inventor's distrust of government was sparked when the British Admiralty refused to pay him for his design of a two-screw propeller, which was demonstrated in 1836 on a ship built in England. The Admiralty argued that a rival inventor had already patented the propeller. Soon after, Ericsson was befriended by Robert F. Stockton, a captain of the United States Navy, who wanted a ship built with Ericsson's propeller. Ericsson designed the ship to Stockton's specifications and named it for the American. Convinced by his new friend that there would be a better market for his designs in the United States, Ericsson sailed his ship – the first of its kind to cross the Atlantic Ocean – to New York City in 1839.

Ericsson's fortunes improved in New York. He met industrialist Cornelius DeLamater, who put him to work in the DeLamater Iron Works and funded his experiments. Ericsson moved into a house not far from the foundry, in lower Manhattan. Between 1840 and 1850, he built two small steamships and twenty-four other boats of various sizes powered by his engines and propellers. But his most ambitious project, started shortly after his arrival in New York, was a propeller-driven steam warship for the U.S. Navy – a contract Stockton helped to secure.

The ship took nearly three years to complete, during which the relationship between Ericsson and Stockton grew increasingly tense. The USS *Princeton*, named for Stockton's New Jersey hometown, was built in the Philadelphia Navy Yard and launched on September 5, 1843. It sailed to Washington in early 1844, captained by Stockton, to perform in trials and demonstrations for eager politicians and military officials. The *Princeton* mastered most tests, including a race with the British steamer SS *Great Western* which she won handily. But on February 28, something went terribly wrong.

About 400 distinguished guests were on board - including President John Tyler, his Cabinet, and former first lady Dolley Madison – for a cruise down the Potomac when a demonstration was called for of the *Princeton*'s firing power. The warship had been fitted with two experimental guns: the Oregon and the Peacemaker. When fired, the Peacemaker exploded, spraying shrapnel into the crowd. Six people were killed, including Secretary of State Abel P. Upshur and Secretary of the Navy Thomas W. Gilmer; twenty others were injured.

Stockton turned on Ericsson and made him the scapegoat of the tragedy; the friendship and partnership devolved into a bitter rivalry, with Stockton continuously opposing the inventor's enterprises. Ericsson vowed never again to deal with Washington.

That first summer of the Civil War was an especially fretful one for Navy Department officials in Washington. Lincoln had ordered a blockade of all Southern ports, but the Navy was hampered by a lack of ships to carry out his order.

In April 1861, fearing Virginia rebels would capture the Norfolk Navy Shipyard, commander Charles Steward McCauley ordered the facility burned and abandoned. In their haste, the Union officers left before the job was done, allowing Confederate raiders to claim a tremendous amount of war material, including 1,195 heavy guns. The Confederacy put to good use even the wreckage. The burned-out wooden hull of the USS *Merrimack* had been salvaged and was being used to construct an ironclad ship. Spies conveyed the news to panicked U.S. Navy officers.

The French and British Royal Navy had been experimenting since 1859 with warships whose hulls were protected by iron plates. The first of these, France's *Gloire* had been launched that November. But no such ship existed in the United States in 1861. The navy that had one of these virtually impregnable ironclads could wreak havoc on the traditional wooden fighting ships. And an ironclad loosed from the Norfolk shipyard would be in a position to win the Civil War. The Navy yard, near the entrance to Chesapeake Bay, controlled the James River approach to Richmond, the Potomac River approach to Washington, and the port of Baltimore.

The Confederates would christen their ironclad warship the CSS *Virginia*; in many historical accounts, it was still known by its Union name, despite bearing no resemblance to the original *Merrimack*. A flag officer named French Forrest was in charge of the salvage operation. He had the wreck towed into the shipyard's only graving dock, where the burned structures were removed. The ship's hull was cut down to just below the water line, where there were no signs of damage. Her engines were intact. The ship's top was envisioned by lieutenants John Mercer Brooke and John L. Porter as a casemate ironclad. It looked like a primitive submarine - a long iron-plated superstructure with slanted sides and ports for ten guns, and a four-foot cast-iron prow affixed to her bow for ramming.

Construction on the CSS *Virginia* was ordered by Confederate States Navy Secretary Stephen Mallory in July 1861. On July 4, Mallory's counterpart in the U.S. Navy, Gideon Welles, suggested to a special session of Congress that a board be appointed to investigate the feasibility of building one or more ironclad steamers or floating batteries. His recommendation became the Ironclad Bill.

Contractors and iron interests descended on Washington. One of the foremost lobbyists, shipbuilder and railroad executive Cornelius Bushnell persuaded the chairman of the Naval Committee to get behind the Ironclad Bill and push it through the House. Congress approved the bill on August 3 and authorized Welles to appoint a board of "three skillful officers." If the board reported favorably, the congressmen decided, $1.5 million could be put toward construction of an ironclad warship. The race was on – but the Union side was already far behind.

Lincoln had appointed Rear Admiral Hiram Paulding, a sixty-four-year-old hero of the War of 1812, to "put the navy afloat." Paulding had been sent to the Norfolk shipyard in April to evacuate Union ships, but finding the Merrimack already in flames, had left it. Paulding was named to Welles's Ironclad Board, and given the responsibility of approving the design of a warship to face the one he had lost. He joined Commodore Joseph Smith, chief of the Bureau of Yards and Docks; and Commander Charles Henry Davis, who also served on Lincoln's Blockade Strategy Board.

The Ironclad Board's first move was to issue, on August 7, a "public appeal to the mechanical ingenuity of our country." A deadline was set, a week later, for contractors to express interest; within a month, those chosen were expected to submit detailed plans - proposed speed, cost, and building time - for an ironclad warship.

E. S. Renwick of New York promised a 6,250-ton giant, 400 feet long, that would move at 18 knots and cost $1.5 million. Donald McKay, famed builder of the world's fastest clipper ships, wanted to spend $1 million and nine months building his version. Cornelius Bushnell submitted plans for his ship, the *Galena*. Sixteen contractors turned in proposals; John Ericsson was not one of them.

While staying at The Willard Hotel in Washington that August, Bushnell shared his idea for the ironclad *Galena* with the ironworks magnate Cornelius DeLamater, who was also in the capital to lobby Congress. DeLamater suggested that Bushnell consult his friend and employee, Ericsson. Bushnell agreed and went to New York City.

When Ann, the elderly maid, opened the door, Bushnell found Ericsson sitting on a revolving piano stool in a combined bedroom-workroom. Bushnell left him the *Galena* plans to study and, returning the next day, was assured they were all right. Ericsson volunteered to show plans of his own and a pasteboard model that he had worked on in 1858. The design showed a turreted ironclad, riding low in the water, with two large guns mounted in a revolving roundhouse.

Bushnell was impressed, and showed the plans to Gideon Welles, who was visiting Hartford. The Navy secretary was equally impressed, and with Bushnell, managed to convince the reluctant Ericsson to present the plans to the Ironclad Board. Bushnell returned to Washington, where the board was still in deliberation.

With the deadline for proposals passed, Bushnell needed help to sway the board to make an exception. He called on two business associates, John A. Griswold, president of the Troy City Bank, and iron-plate manufacturer John F. Winslow. Bushnell offered them a quarter interest each in the ironclad if Ericsson's design was awarded the contract. Together, the men approached Ironclad Board member Commodore Joseph Smith, who was unimpressed. Bushnell went higher – straight to Lincoln.

Secretary of State William H. Seward set up Bushnell's meeting with the president. Lincoln heard the ironclad proposal and agreed to a meeting in Commodore Smith's office the next day. Lincoln attended, along with Gustavus Vasa Fox - the dynamic new, and first, assistant secretary of the Navy - Bushnell, Griswold, Winslow, Commodore Paulding, and Commander Davis. Nearly all admitted that Ericsson's plan was novel. But Davis thought it was silly and ridiculed it. Smith was noncommittal. Lincoln listened for an hour, and then in closing the meeting, remarked: "All I can say is what the girl said when she put her foot in the stocking: 'I think there's something in it.'" Ericsson's floating battery, soon to be known as the USS *Monitor*, became the seventeenth entry.

On September 16, the Ironclad Board eliminated fourteen of the proposals - including McKay's because it was too slow, and Renwick's eighteen-knot giant because it was too costly. Still in the running were the *Galena*, a design by Philadelphia builders Merrick & Sons called New Ironsides, and Ericsson's *Monitor*, at the top of the list. The next day, Davis prevailed in having the *Monitor* crossed off.

Bushnell refused to give up on the plan. He pressed board members Paulding and Smith, who agreed to support the Ericsson design, but only if Davis could also be convinced. Davis remained opposed, telling Bushnell he "might take the little model home and worship it, as it would not be idolatry, because it was made in the image of nothing in heaven above, or the earth below, or in the waters under the earth."

There was only one thing left for Bushnell to do: Bring Ericsson to Washington to confront Davis in person. As he set off for New York, Smith helped by writing to Ericsson that there "seemed to be some deficiencies in the specifications . . . some changes may be suggested . . . [and] a guarantee would be required."

Convinced by Bushnell that Davis merely wanted a few points clarified, Ericsson took a train to Washington. On meeting Davis, the inventor declared, "I have come down at the suggestion of Captain Bushnell, to explain about the plan of the *Monitor.*"

"What," queried Davis, "the little plan Bushnell had here Tuesday? Why, we rejected it in toto."

"Rejected it! What for . . . ?"

"For want of stability. . . ."

"Stability," exclaimed Ericsson. "No craft that ever

floated was more stable than she would be; that is one of her great merits."

Davis, softening, answered: "Prove it . . . and we will recommend it at once."

Ericsson agreed to a presentation to the board that afternoon and offered two hours of evidence that his designs were sound. "The sea shall ride over her and she shall live in it like a duck," he said. The board members deliberated for two more hours, at the end of which they notified Gideon Welles that they were satisfied. Welles called Ericsson to his office late that afternoon and told him to get started immediately; the contract could be signed later. Ericsson rushed back to the ironworks in New York.

Investors Griswold and Winslow, looking for someone to build the *Monitor,* boarded a ferry in lower Manhattan and crossed the East River to the heart of the Greenpoint shipbuilding industry. They met Thomas Fitch Rowland, the proprietor of Continental Iron Works and asked how much he would charge per pound to build an iron ship for them. Rowland was experienced in making big things, having once manufactured a quarter-mile-long iron pipe, seven-and-a-half feet in diameter, for New York City's Croton aqueduct. After some negotiating, the price was set at seven-and-a-half cents per pound of iron.

The government contract, signed October 4 by Ericsson and his associates, said: "It is further agreed between the said parties that said vessel and equipment in all respects shall be completed and ready for sea in one hundred days from the date of this indenture." A small-print clause stated that if the vessel - "an Iron-Clad-Shot-Proof Steam Battery of iron and wood" - was not a success, Ericsson's group would have to issue a full refund to the government.

Bushnell emphasized to Commodore Smith what a good bargain he was getting: "The whole vessel with her equipment will cost no more than to maintain one regiment in the field twelve months. . . . (yet) will it not be of infinitely more service than 100 regiments?"

Bargain or not, the *Monitor* started at a disadvantage. The Confederate shipbuilders already had a hull, boilers, and engines for their CSS *Virginia*, though the iron sheathing for the ship's sloping deckhouse was not yet ready.

The Union had to mobilize capital, planners, manufacturers, and shipbuilders into a fast-working team. The nerve center was Ericsson's room on Franklin Street. Iron tycoon Griswold took charge of the finances. While Rowland built the hull, the revolving turret - the most innovative of the *Monitor*'s features – was to be fabricated at the Novelty Iron Works of New York. Machinery, boiler, and turret-turning apparatus would be made in the DeLamater Iron Works, and the iron plates rolled out by the Albany Iron Works in Troy. Gunport shields for the turret were the work of Buffalo ironworker Charles D. Delaney.

Winslow was responsible for expediting materials shipped out of Albany. "One hundred days, and they are short ones, are few enough to do all that is to be done," he declared. He wanted the hull-plate specifications immediately because "the making of slabs is the longest part of the operation." On October 12, eight days after the contract was signed in Washington, Winslow wrote Ericsson: "I am now able to say that every bar of angle iron is now made and ready to go on board of Monday's steamer and be in New York on Tuesday morning. On Tuesday another lot will follow and so on daily until the entire order for hull plates is completed. We shall drive them energetically . . . until you will cry HOLD! in mercy."

At the Continental Iron Works, with its many buildings sprawled over a city block from the East River inland, Rowland built a ship house large enough to accommodate the *Monitor's* 172-foot-long, forty-one-foot-wide armored raft and the supporting hull. He made a model of the ship to determine the exact size of the armor plates needed, and numbered the plates in sequence so when they arrived they could be assembled without refitting. On October 19, he estimated the cost of the woodwork at $11,287. A week later, he laid the keel, and the furnaces of the Continental Iron Works were fired up.

Ericsson planned, drew, and superintended incessantly. He took the ferry to the shipyard daily. In the early morning and late evening, he drafted the hundreds of detailed plans at his office. The blueprints flowed directly from him to the various shops, and as soon as the material arrived, each piece was manufactured. If it wasn't right, he was there to adjust it. He made his designs as simple as possible to speed up the work. "The magnitude of the work I have to do," he said, "exceeds anything I have ever before undertaken."

Smith was also an active manager. Before the keel was laid, Smith was already worrying about the ventilation, writing that "sailors do not fancy living under water without breathing in sunshine occasionally." He also didn't like the plan for the rudder. Ericsson reassured him: "I beg you to rest tranquil as to the result; success cannot fail to crown the undertaking." But when, the day after the keel was laid, Smith wanted to know how a five-foot-eight man could stand in a five-foot-high pilothouse, Ericsson bristled, "It is an unpleasant task continually to contradict the opinions you express."

Another challenge arose at the DeLamater Iron Works. "The motive engine," said Ericsson, "is somewhat peculiar, consisting of only one steam cylinder with pistons at opposite ends, a steam tight partition being introduced in the middle. The propeller shaft has only one crank and one crank pin." Even if it did get made right, Ericsson worried, who would be able to operate it? He believed the only man for the job was Alban C. Stimers, who two years before had been chief engineer on the USS *Merrimack*. Ericsson asked for him, and Commodore Smith wrote that Stimers would arrive in a week. By then, it was November.

Directly across Manhattan from DeLamater's plant, the turret was taking shape at the Novelty Iron Works. It was twenty feet in diameter, nine feet high, and with sides eight inches thick, made of eight layers of iron plates. The job required an industrial plant capable of the heaviest kind of work, and Novelty was up to it. Its main building was 206 feet long and eighty feet wide, housing four furnaces and six drying ovens.

As large as the turret was, the builders struggled to make room for the crew and especially for the recoil of the eleven-inch Dahlgren guns. "I must insist," said Smith, "on the guns having the full length of recoil." Stimers said the guns would have to be shortened. But Admiral John Dahlgren, said to do so would reduce the guns' effectiveness by 50 percent. Smith would not allow it. Novelty Iron

Works forged ahead, building tracks in the turret for two gun carriages.

In Buffalo, construction of the gunport shields was progressing more smoothly. Delaney designed the shields to swing, pendulum-like, to close the ports when the guns were retracted into the turret, thus protecting the crew.

By November 18, the *Monitor*'s designs were public knowledge. Smith wrote: "I received the copies of the *Scientific American* and regret to see a description of the vessel in print before she shall have been tested." The commodore was concerned, and rightly so, that the report would reach Norfolk and speed up the Confederates' ironclad. But the press was not all flattering: Critics, led by Ericsson's former partner Stockton, began to deride the *Monitor* project as "Ericcson's Folly" and the "Yankee cheesebox."

Work continued steadily as government dollars poured in; the first payment of $37,500 was made around Thanksgiving, and another $50,000 installment arrived in December. Secretary of the Navy Welles, in his annual report on December 2, said the Ironclad Board had "displayed great practical wisdom" in this new branch of naval architecture. But Smith was not relaxing one bit. He sent a terse warning to Ericsson on December 5 to "push up the work . . . only thirty-nine days left."

At the Continental Iron Works, Rowland's men bolted armor on the side and deck of the *Monitor* amid rumors that spies had infiltrated the shipyard and were passing information to Richmond.

January of 1862 was the critical month, with the 100-day deadline approaching. The gun problem had not yet been solved. A strike at the Brooklyn Navy Yard, where the *Monitor* would have to be fitted out, threatened more delays. New Year's Day started out with a gale that tore the USS *North Carolina*, then training the *Monitor*'s crew, away from the pier and bashed in her stern.

The first week of 1862 was hardly out before drifting ice filled up the East River, blocked the Brooklyn waterfront, and backed up into Bushwick Creek bordering on the Continental Iron Works. Three days before the *Monitor* was supposed to launch, outside work in shipyards had to be suspended because of stormy weather.

On January 14, Smith wrote Ericsson to remind him that "the time for the completion of the shot-proof battery . . . expired on January 12th." Smith was right; the federal contract had been signed by the government exactly 100 days before. But the government did nothing about cancelation; it wanted the *Monitor* under almost any terms. Moreover, the government was partly responsible for the delay since it had not yet been able to provide the guns.

Practical details were worked out. Ericsson proposed that the ship, up to this point referred to as Ericsson's Battery, be called the *Monitor*. Lieutenant Samuel Dana Greene was assigned as executive officer. Rowland, preparing for the launch, asked Ericsson to send riggers to assist, and constructed wooden boxes to buoy the ship's stern should she plow too deep in the water upon leaving the ramp.

Smith forwarded the news that the *Virginia* had been floated out of dry dock on January 25 and urged Ericsson to hold the *Monitor*'s trials as soon as possible.

The *Monitor* moved out of its ship house at 9:45 a.m. on January 30, gathered momentum, and slipped down the ramp into the East River. The Stars and Stripes flew from the turret and flagstaff. Tugboats, puffing black smoke and white steam, stood by to help. Ericsson, Lieutenant Greene, and Acting Volunteer Master Louis N. Stodder stood on deck while a top-hatted crowd watched from the shore. It was the 101st working day from the date the contract was signed and the 100th day from the laying of the keel.

The Brooklyn Daily Eagle reported the next day a "highly successful" launch, and described the *Monitor* as "broad and flat-bottomed, with vertical sides and pointed ends, requiring but a very small low depth of water to float in, though heavily loaded with an impregnable armor upon its sides and a bomb-proof deck, on which is placed a shot-proof revolving turret, that will contain two very heavy guns." The vessel, the article concluded, "will soon be ready for a trial trip, when some idea can be formed as to her usefulness."

Fox sent Ericsson a telegram on the launching day to "hurry her to sea as the *Merrimack* is nearly ready at Norfolk."

The *Monitor*'s gun problem was soon solved. An ordnance officer at the Brooklyn Navy Yard was authorized to take two eleven-inch guns out of the gunboat *Dacotah*. On February 5, the guns were mounted in the *Monitor*'s turret, "presenting a formidable appearance." Four days later, the main engine was turned over.

At last, on February 19, DeLamater's mechanics lit the fires in the boilers and warmed up the engines. Ericsson boarded the *Monitor*, and it made its way into the river for its first trial trip - in a blinding snowstorm. There were other complications: A number of valves had been installed backward, and the vessel could not get up to speed. The valves were adjusted, and that same evening, as the snow changed to rain, Thomas Rowland delivered the *Monitor* to Hiram Paulding at the Brooklyn Navy Yard.

In Hampton Roads, the Union's Admiral Louis M. Goldsborough, commander of the North Atlantic

Blockading Squadron, had a motley array of vessels - old sailing frigates, steamers, and tugs - and all were in danger. The CSS *Virginia* could sink them at will and, it was feared, proceed north and attack New York Harbor.

On February 20, Welles sent sailing orders to the *Monitor*'s captain, John Lorimer Worden, a veteran naval officer who had recently been incarcerated as a Confederate prisoner of war: "Proceed with the U.S. Steamer *Monitor* under your command to Hampton Roads, Va." But in his haste, Welles had forgotten that the *Monitor* had yet to be commissioned. There was no crew on board, no provisions, no ammunition, and its battery had not been tested.

The next day, a messenger from the American Telegraph Company sped to Ericsson's office on Franklin Street, bearing an envelope addressed to "J. Ericsson, Constructor of Iron Battery." Opening it, Ericsson read:

> It is very important that you should say exactly the day the *Monitor* can be at Hampton Roads. Consult with Comdr. Paulding.
>
> G. V. FOX
>
> Ass't Sec'y Navy

A new underwater cable from Fortress Monroe to

Cape Charles meant news of Confederate actions reached the North twelve to twenty hours sooner. Rebel Secretary Mallory had named a commanding officer for his new ironclad: Captain Franklin Buchanan, who had been the first superintendent of the Naval Academy at Annapolis and had commanded the Washington Navy Yard. But the *Virginia* still had not been loaded with ammunition.

On February 25, the *Monitor* was commissioned at the Brooklyn Navy Yard. The crew marched from the USS *North Carolina*, and skidded down the gangway sloping from the pier to the iron deck of their new ship, floating barely eighteen inches above the river. All that was visible was the turret, the tiny pilothouse near the bow, and two small vents at the other end. Worden ordered the flag hoisted and read his orders, as the crew loaded provisions and ammunition. The *Monitor* was at last a ship of the United States Navy. Ericsson telegraphed Gustavus Fox that the *Monitor* would depart the next day.

It was snowing heavily on February 26 as the *Monitor* sailed down the East River for the Narrows and the open sea. Bushnell, writing from The Willard in Washington, had "no doubt of her making a good and safe passage to the entire satisfaction of all parties." But steering became difficult, and by the time the *Monitor* was abreast of Wall Street, only a mile downstream, it was clear she could not continue. Worden reluctantly gave the order to turn around, and the *Monitor* returned to the Navy Yard.

Rowland said he could put the *Monitor* in the sectional dock at the foot of Pike Street "with perfect safety, alter her rudder, and have her out in twenty-four hours." But Ericsson, annoyed, said it was unnecessary to dock the ship, and made the adjustment himself.

The Confederates, too, had been delayed. Flag Officer French Forrest, commandant of the Norfolk Navy Yard, was desperate for gunpowder for the *Virginia*, but it would take three days to fill the ship's cartridge boxes.

On March 4, Captain Worden took the *Monitor* into the open sea off Sandy Hook for a final trial. The two eleven-inch guns were loaded with fifteen-pound powder charges and shot weighing 168 pounds, the gunport shields swung aside, and the carriages ran out on their rails until the gun muzzles protruded from the ship's sides. They were fired time and again. The new turning mechanism, which had caused Ericsson so much trouble, pivoted the twenty-foot turret smoothly.

The *Monitor* returned triumphantly to the yard at 5:00 that evening. Smith was pleased enough to send a payment for $18,750. But there still was a great deal of work to do. Sailing date was set for

March 6; Greene did not see how the ship could possibly make it.

Paulding ordered the steamers *Currituck* and *Sachem* to stand by to escort the *Monitor* to Hampton Roads, and a tug to take her in tow. Another storm was approaching.

About 11:00 a.m. on March 6, the *Monitor* left the Brooklyn Navy Yard in a light westerly breeze. Opposite Governor's Island, the tug took her in tow. Soon, the *Monitor* disappeared from view, heading south.

The sea turned angry on March 7, and the *Monitor* suffered. Water poured down through the turret foundations and into the boiler room. Men in the engine room nearly suffocated and had to be dragged out. The engine stopped, and Worden ordered the ship towed close to the coast, where there would be calmer water. Five hours were lost.

At Norfolk, it had been a trying day for the Confederacy. Although the Stars and Bars were run up on the CSS *Virginia*, the crew was worried the ship was not prepared for the heavy work she had to do. The engines had not been tested. And trials had revealed a weakness at the waterline. Some crew members predicted total failure; few expected to return to Norfolk.

That evening, the *Monitor* sailed again, prodded by chief engineer Alban Stimers despite the discouragement of the crew, which was exhausted, choked with fumes and soaked.

The morning of Sunday, March 8, dawned quietly for Goldsborough's blockade squadron, anchored at Hampton Roads. Hardly a ripple disturbed the surface of the bay as the U.S. Navy admiral engaged his men in dull routine. Goldsborough had waited so long for the Confederate ironclad and heard so many false alarms, that he had been lulled into a false sense of security. At Newport News, the fifty-gun frigate USS *Congress*, commanded by Joseph B. Smith, the commodore's son, waited. Nearby was the *Cumberland*, and by Old Point Comfort, the remainder of the squadron headed by Van Brunt's steam frigate *Minnesota*. Gustavus Fox left Washington for Fortress Monroe, guarding Hampton Roads, to see how the *Monitor* would make out.

Just before 11:00 a.m., the CSS *Virginia's* quick-tempered captain ordered the vessel to sail. The ship set out so abruptly that workmen had to jump ashore while in motion. Rebel crowds cheered. Laboring against a strong flood tide, the *Virginia* steamed down the Elizabeth River and into Hampton Roads at her top speed of six knots, escorted by the gunboats *Raleigh* and *Beaufort*. Dragging its deep, twenty-two-foot hull through the water, with heavy smoke pouring from its stack, it steered poorly. Buchanan called all hands to quarters and told them, "You shall have no reason to complain of not fighting at close quarters."

Spotting smoke coming down the Elizabeth River, the USS *Cumberland* sent the tug *Zouave* to Pig Point to investigate. The *Zouave* crew saw "what looked to them like the roof of a barn belching forth smoke from a chimney;" it was the *Virginia*. But the Confederate ironclad was hugging the opposite shore so closely and moving so slowly that the Union sailors believed it was conducting a trial run.

At about 4:00 p.m., as the *Monitor* passed Cape Henry and entered the Chesapeake Bay, the crew heard gunfire. The *Virginia* was in the act of destroying the *Congress*, whose captain, Joe Smith, was killed.

A pilot boarded the *Monitor* and told about the havoc the *Virginia* had created in the Union squadron. The *Minneapolis* was aground, the *Congress* on fire, and the *Cumberland* had sunk. The *Monitor* rushed to the battle area, but it was too late. The victorious *Virginia* had already gone to port. The *Monitor* anchored alongside the *Minnesota* to wait for dawn.

By 8:00 p.m., the *Virginia* was anchored off Sewall's Point. She had lost her prow but was otherwise in fighting trim. Her exhausted crew had to clear away the debris of battle before the cooks could prepare a meal. Then, the men stayed up to watch the fire they had started near Newport News. Shortly after midnight, the *Congress* blew up, and the Confederates turned in. But they were soon up again, raising anchor at 6:20 a.m.

Less than two hours later, the *Virginia* and the *Monitor* met in the first battle between ironclads. The *Virginia*, accompanied by several steamers, headed toward the *Minnesota*, firing at the Union vessel which had been run aground the previous day. Aboard the *Monitor*, Captain Worden gave the order to commence firing.

Five times, the two ironclads came so close to each other that they touched, and on both, the armor proved formidable. After two hours of combat, the *Monitor* broke away briefly to give her crew time to hoist shot into the turret. When the battle was joined again half an hour later, the pilothouse on the *Monitor* was struck. Worden, temporarily blinded by the impact, turned over command to Greene.

Stimers ordered the turret guns to keep firing, until suddenly the *Virginia* - running out of fuel, riding high at the bow, and leaking - broke off contact and headed toward Sewall's Point. Greene did not pursue; instead, he turned the *Monitor* toward the *Minnesota*, guarding the support ship until it could get back out to sea.

The four-and-a-half hour battle ended in a stand-off, but for all intents it was a Union victory. As Gideon Welles put it: "There is no reason to believe that any of our wooden vessels guarding the Southern Coast would have withstood [the *Virginia's*] attacks any better than the *Cumberland*, *Congress*, or *Minnesota*. She might have ascended the Potomac, and thrown bombshells into the Capitol of the Union. In short, it is difficult to assign limits to her destructive power. But for the timely arrival of the *Monitor* . . . our whole fleet of wooden ships, and probably the whole sea coast, would have been at the mercy of a terrible assailant."

In May, when the Confederates evacuated Norfolk, they decided the *Virginia* was too unseaworthy for the open ocean and drew too much water to make it up the James River to Richmond, so its own crew destroyed the ship. The *Monitor*, with Greene still aboard, was towed to blockade duty off Beaufort, North Carolina, where it foundered off Cape Hatteras during a storm on December 31, 1862.

John Ericsson continued to build ironclads for the Union navy for the remainder of the war, but the building of the *Monitor* had made him the hero of the "hundred-day miracle."

10
PRISON CAMPS OF
THE CIVIL WAR
– BRUCE CATTON

On November 10, 1865, Henry Wirz - a pale, black-whiskered, used-up captain in the used-up army of the Confederate States of America - walked through a door in the Old Capitol Prison at Washington, climbed thirteen wooden steps, and stood under the crossbeam of a scaffold with a greased noose around his neck.

A Union Army major stood on the platform next to him. Wirz turned, extended his hand, and offered his pardon for the thing which his executioner was about to do.

"I know what orders are, major," said Wirz. "I am being hung for obeying them."

The two men shook hands and drew apart. The drop was sprung; Wirz, a black mask over his face and leather straps binding his arms and legs, dangled at the end of a rope and died. Across the northern part of the recently reunited United States, many celebrated the death sentence of a villain.

By modern standards, Wirz may have been considered a war criminal. But more accurately, he was a scapegoat, singled out to die on the altar of history for the sins of many – both north and south of the Potomac River.

Wirz had been commandant of Andersonville Prison, the hideous institution established in February 1864 by the collapsing Confederacy to hold Union prisoners of war. Of the more than 30,000 Union prisoners kept there, some 12,000 died. When the war ended, the public looked to punish someone; Wirz was the easy choice.

Wirz was born in Switzerland and studied medicine at the University of Zurich. He emigrated to America in 1849 after the death of his first wife, with whom he had two children. In Kentucky, he established a medical practice and married a Methodist widow who had two daughters of her own. The family moved to Louisville, where it grew by one more. By 1861, he was a successful doctor.

Wirz enlisted in a Louisiana volunteer regiment after the fall of Fort Sumter in April 1861. At the

Battle of Seven Pines in May 1862, he was shot in the right arm. Wirz returned to his unit in June and was promoted to captain "for bravery on the field of battle." In 1863, he asked for leave to go to Europe, where he thought he could get better medical treatment for his injury. Jefferson Davis sent him with secret dispatches to Confederate sympathizers in London and France. Wirz stayed for a year and underwent a failed operation that left his right arm useless. The captain, who was brusque to begin with, grew irritable and snappish.

Returning to the Confederacy, Wirz was assigned to the staff of General John H. Winder, who was in charge of the prison camps. He served briefly as a prison guard – first in Alabama, then Richmond. In April 1864, he was given command of the prison camp at Andersonville.

Early in the war, the two governments signed a cartel, providing that, at frequent intervals, prisoners would be exchanged on a man-for-man basis. There was an intricate table of values - a lieutenant was worth a certain number of privates, a colonel was worth a larger number, and so on. Many prisoners had to wait a long time to be exchanged, but this system kept the prisoner-of-war population on both sides fairly stable and manageable.

In 1863, the exchange system began to collapse. When Ulysses S. Grant became general in chief of the Union armies, he surveyed the cartel with a realistic eye. By this time, there were more Confederate prisoners in the North than there were Union prisoners in the South. Because the Confederacy needed manpower more than the Union, Grant concluded the cessation of exchange hurt the South and helped the North. Thus, the sacrifice of prisoners was necessary to bring Union victory nearer.

The population of Northern and Southern prison camps began to grow, and the camps became places of hardship, suffering, and death. Throughout the war, the North held about 215,000 Confederate prisoners, and the South about 194,000 Unionists. Of these, 24,436 died in the Northern camps, and 22,576 in the Southern camps. Another statistic offers some perspective of the scale of the prison camp horrors: The camps held more than twice the number of soldiers who fought in the Battle of Gettysburg - and killed nearly ten times as many.

Each side suspected the other of mistreating and killing prisoners, but little more than human clumsiness was involved. In all of the work and responsibilities of war, the prison camps usually came last. After manning and supplying the army, keeping the economy going, feeding and clothing the home front – then whatever time, money, energy, and administrative competence was left was applied to the care of prisoners. This was not nearly enough, on either side.

The site for Andersonville Prison was selected because it was far enough from the battle lines to provide security, and large enough to accommodate prisoners who would have to be removed from places dangerously near the advancing Union armies. A sixteen-and-a-half acre enclosure was set up in a rolling meadow crossed by a little stream, and a stockade was built around it.

The first prisoners arrived before the stockade was finished and before there were any barracks or huts. Soon 400 prisoners were arriving every day. By May, 15,000 prisoners were crammed into the enclosure which had been designed to accommodate 10,000.

The situation was out of hand when Wirz took over. Prisoners had no housing, except for foxholes and makeshift tents assembled from blankets, tree branches, and scraps of wood. The authorities had no axes, spades, shovels, picks, or other tools and found it almost impossible to get any. A Confederate colonel reported that he lacked even implements to dig graves. It was late in May before the camp had tools sufficient for digging drainage ditches to keep the little stream unpolluted.

By midsummer, Wirz had managed to enlarge the stockade by ten acres, but there were 30,000 prisoners and the prison was little better than a quagmire. A Confederate officer who inspected the camp in August reported there was just enough room to provide six square feet of ground for each prisoner, and men were dying at the rate of 100 a day.

The real problem was beyond Wirz's control: The Confederate economy, ground down by four years of war, was collapsing, which made maintaining a decent prison for 30,000 men impossible. Trees near the prison were abundant, but the manpower, money, and equipment needed to turn them into lumber and then into buildings was lacking.

Georgia had a surplus of food, but the railroads were breaking down, and Confederate armies were going hungry. A government that could not feed its soldiers was not going to give much food to its war prisoners. The inmates at Andersonville got mostly corn meal, made out of corn with the cobs ground in unsifted. Without wood or proper utensils to cook it, about a third of the prisoners died of scurvy or dysentery – their emaciated bodies dumped into mass graves.

Malnutrition and disease were not all that killed the prisoners. Some tried to escape, only to be shot by sentries perched in pigeon roosts as they approached a log fence inside the stockade wall known as the dead line. Others fell victim to fellow prisoners who called themselves Andersonville Raiders, gangsters and thieves armed with clubs. Another group of prisoners, the Regulators led by Big Pete Aubrey, exacted their own justice inside the prison, hanging six of the Raiders with Wirz's approval. Eighteen other gangsters who escaped hanging were beaten so badly that three of them died.

Gangs plagued Andersonville. One of the prisoners, Connecticut Volunteer Robert H. Kellogg, survived to describe his first impressions of the camp. "As we entered the place, a spectacle met our eyes that almost froze our blood with horror, and made our hearts fail within us," Kellogg wrote. "Before us were forms that had once been active and erect – stalwart men, now nothing more but mere walking skeletons, covered with filth and vermin. Many of our men, in the heat and intensity of their feeling, exclaimed with earnestness, 'Can this be hell? God protect us!' and all thought that He alone could bring them out alive from so terrible a place. In the center of the whole was a swamp, occupying about three or four acres of the narrowed limits, and a part of this marshy place had been used by the prisoners as a sink, and excrement covered the ground, the scent arising from which was suffocating. The ground allotted to our ninety was near the edge of this plague-spot, and how we were to live through the warm summer weather in the midst of such fearful surroundings was more than we cared to think just then."

Exasperated by the nearly impossible task of keeping the prisoners alive, Captain Wirz tried a different tactic. In June 1864, he pardoned five Union soldiers and sent them North with a petition to reinstate prisoner exchanges. The petition was denied, and the soldiers carried the news back to Andersonville. That same summer, a Catholic priest from Savannah, Father Peter Whelan, arrived at the camp. He stayed for four months, ministering to the sick and utilizing the church's resources to bring in clothes and food. The prisoners called him the Angel of Andersonville. Before he left, he borrowed $16,000 in Confederate money to buy 10,000 pounds of wheat flour, had it baked into bread, and distributed at the prison hospital.

Early in the fall of 1864, the warring governments worked out a deal to exchange prisoners who were too sick to be put back into combat. The prison authorities at Elmira culled out 1,200 such men and put them on a train for Baltimore, where they would take a ship to some Southern port. Union doctors who met the train protested that many of the men were in no condition to travel; five had died on the train, and sixty more had to be sent to a hospital as soon as they got to Baltimore. The doctors accused the prison authorities of criminal neglect and inhumanity. The commander of the Elmira camp wrote that even though he had sent away 1,200 of his worst cases, his hospital soon was as crowded as ever, with a fearful death rate.

When the war ended, Andersonville became

a symbol of the needless suffering the war had caused. The prison was captured by Union forces in May 1865. Wirz was arrested, imprisoned, and on August 21, 1865, went on trial before a military commission in Washington. He was charged with conspiring with Confederate officers to weaken or kill Union prisoners, and with murder "in violation of the laws and customs of war." The press characterized Wirz as "the Andersonville savage," "the inhuman wretch," and "the infamous captain," and his leading attorney remarked that Wirz was doomed before he even got a hearing.

The military court heard a vast amount of evidence about horrible conditions at the prison, passed lightly over evidence that Wirz had tried without success to get these conditions bettered, and refused to hear any testimony indicating Northern prison camps were not much better. The trial lasted nearly two months. Father Whelan spoke on Wirz's behalf, but the priest's testimony was trumped by survivors who claimed to have seen the commander kick prisoners to death and shoot others. Wirz was convicted of conspiracy and all but two of thirteen counts of murder. He wrote to President Andrew Johnson to plead for clemency, but Johnson refused to intervene.

The night before he was to die for his crimes, Wirz was supposedly approached in his cell with a proposition. A high Cabinet official, he was told, could get his sentence commuted if Wirz would implicate Confederate President Jefferson Davis in the atrocities at Andersonville. Wirz replied: ". . . I do not know anything about Jefferson Davis. He had no connection with . . . what was done at Andersonville. . . . I would not become a traitor against him or anybody else even to save my own life."

Wirz faced his fate alone on November 10, 1865. Led into the courtyard at Old Capitol Prison, he stopped at the door of a fellow prisoner and asked him to take care of his wife and children. Then he went on to meet his death with a composure which moved *Leslie's Illustrated* (which had denounced him during his trial) to remark that there was "something in his face and step which, in a better man, might have passed for heroism."

Andersonville remained a reproach for years to come - a favorite topic during the 1880s and 1890s for Northern political candidates who campaigned by "waving the bloody shirt." But with the passage of years emerged a new perspective: Andersonville as a creation of its time and place, and the real culprit was not Wirz, the luckless scapegoat, but war itself.

11
THE ROCK OF
CHICKAMAUGA
– PETER ANDREWS

The most consistently underrated and overlooked of all the Civil War's military commanders is General George Henry Thomas, the big Virginia cavalryman who fought for the Union. From January 1862 at Mill Springs, where he won the first major Union victory of the war, through December 1864 at Nashville, where he destroyed the Army of Tennessee, Thomas never lost a battle when he was in command.

Thomas took scraps of units from a beaten army, pulled them into a defensive perimeter, held the line at Chickamauga, and saved the Western command in September 1863, earning him the nickname "The Rock of Chickamauga." Two months later, at Chattanooga, Thomas's Army of the Cumberland put the Union in position to break the rebellion with one of the most stunning assaults in military history.

Thomas won many honors and promotions, and in Washington, a statue of him sits atop a horse in bronze. Still, his fame, one historian said, "never really caught up with his talents." Thomas is partially to blame for this lack of recognition; he never really wanted it. He once said he would not have his life "hawked about in print for the amusement of the curious." He was one of the few field commanders in the Union army who did not write their memoirs or publish their papers. Thomas was still on active service when he died, and the task of honoring his memory and defending his record fell to secondary hands.

When it came time for dividing credit among his generals, Ulysses Grant was stingy with Thomas. The two never got along. Thomas made Grant uneasy, exuding an aristocratic manner and sometimes ignoring his chief's orders.

The men serving under Thomas were more generous. Nicknames, when freely given, are generally a sign of affection. No one had more than Thomas. He was variously known as Pap, Old Slow Trot, Uncle George, and Old Reliable. His demeanor at West Point was so grave that his fellow cadet William Rosecrans called him General Washington. In something of a failed journalistic overreach, he was also called the Sledge of Nashville.

Six feet tall and weighing more than 200 pounds, Thomas cut a heroic figure. A Chicago journalist said the general appeared "hewn out of a large square block of the best tempered material that men are made of . . . square face, square shoulders, square step; blue eyes, with depths in them, withdrawn beneath a penthouse of a brow." Thomas, the reporter concluded, was "the right kind of man to tie to."

As Rosecrans's nickname for him suggested, George Henry Thomas was the kind of soldier who looked like a future general from the moment he put on his first uniform. In 1840, he graduated twelfth in his class at West Point - six behind William Tecumseh Sherman, his first-year roommate. While Sherman stayed in the ranks, Thomas was made corporal. He earned promotions for bravery in the Second Seminole War, and as one of Zachary Taylor's gunners during the Mexican War.

In 1851, he returned to West Point as an artillery and cavalry instructor, where he established a close professional relationship with another Virginia officer, Robert E. Lee, who was acting then as the academy's superintendent. His students included Jeb Stuart, John Bell Hood, and the superintendent's nephew, Fitzhugh Lee.

At the academy, Thomas picked up one of his more enduring nicknames, Slow Trot. The horses he had to work with at West Point were in poor condition - one was blind, and another suffered from a nervous disorder and kept falling down – and Thomas wouldn't let his students drive their mounts any faster.

In 1855, Thomas was appointed a major of the 2nd U.S. Cavalry, an elite troop assembled by Secretary of War Jefferson Davis. Meant to be a showpiece of the service, the regiment mounted only the best horses, which were color-coordinated so that each troop had animals of complementary hues and was armed with the latest weaponry, including new breech-loading rifles. Davis specially recruited the officers; while it was common to give command of a new regiment to a political appointee, only professionals were considered for this duty. Command was given to Colonel Albert Sidney Johnston, whom Davis had served with in the Mexican War. Johnston's second in command was Lieutenant Colonel Robert E. Lee. William J. Hardee, whose book on tactics would become a standard Army text, was appointed major alongside Thomas. The junior officers included seven future generals: George Stoneman, Richard W. Johnson, and Kenner Garrard, who fought for the Union; and Confederates Hood, Earl Van Dorn, Edmund Kirby Smith, and Fitzhugh Lee.

The 2nd Cavalry was dispatched to the Western frontier, to put down Indian uprisings; there, Thomas received the only combat wound of his long military career. Leading a mounted troop in pursuit of marauding Comanches, Thomas came upon a single man. The Indian hit three soldiers and drove a shaft through Thomas's chin, into his chest. Thomas pulled the arrow out and continued to command until the Comanche was killed.

Thomas made himself into the most meticulous commander of the war. "The fate of an army," he once said, "may depend on a buckle." Unlike generals who prided themselves on being fighters who couldn't be bothered with bureaucracy, Thomas enjoyed paperwork. He made sure his correspondence was up to date before a fight and that no papers were awaiting his signature. On the morning of the Battle of Nashville, Thomas stopped his staff in the street to make arrangements for fourteen bushels of coal to be delivered to a neighbor.

Thomas was a Virginian, and when the Civil War made men choose between their country and their state, he agonized more than most. Nineteen of the thirty-six officers in the 2nd Cavalry resigned to join the Confederacy. A few months before the raid on Fort Sumter, Thomas applied to be commandant of cadets at the Virginia Military Institute. He turned down an offer from Virginia

Governor John Letcher to become chief ordnance officer of the Virginia army. Finally, he wrote his wife, Frances, that he was staying with the Union. "Turn it every way he would," Mrs. Thomas later recalled, the most important consideration was "his duty to the government of the United States."

Coming from a Confederate state and fighting for the Union put Thomas in a difficult position. To the North, he was a Virginia slave owner and, therefore, suspect. His Southern heritage had helped him gain advancement when men such as Jefferson Davis were running the War Department, but now it worked against him. Lincoln once struck his name from a promotions list, saying, "Let the Virginian wait." To the South, however, Thomas was a traitor; his property was confiscated, and his family disowned him. Jeb Stuart, his former student, wrote his wife that "Old George H. Thomas is in command of the cavalry of the enemy. I would like to hang, *hang* him as a traitor to his native state."

Thomas provided the Union with one of its few victories in early 1862, when he was sent to help wrest control of eastern Kentucky from his former colonel, Albert Sidney Johnston. The war had just begun; each side sought out men in their ranks who could lead.

The opening skirmishes had been conducted by two inexperienced generals: Felix Zollicoffer, a Tennessee newspaper editor who had served in Congress, and Union officer Albin Francisco Schoepf. Born in Polish Austria, Schoepf was a graduate of the Vienna military academy and had served in the Prussian army. While Zollicoffer was passionately devoted to the Southern cause, his only military experience consisted of a year's service fighting the Seminoles in 1836. In October 1861, at Wild Cat Mountain in Kentucky, Schoepf's troops first swept Zollicoffer's Confederates aside. But later, under vigorous counterattack, the Union army fled the field in what became known as the Wild Cat Stampede.

The high commands of both sides attempted to bring discipline to the tangled situation. The South installed Major General George Bibb Crittenden over Zollicoffer, and the North brought in Thomas as strike-force commander. Crittenden had the more difficult job; Zollicoffer was as prickly as he was incompetent. He disobeyed Crittenden's order to use the Cumberland Gap as a shield and placed his troops between Thomas and the river. It was no place for a battle, but rather than risk trying to get back across the Cumberland, Crittenden decided to fight. He led his soldiers on a night march through heavy rain, hoping to surprise Thomas in his camp. A daring plan, it might well have worked against a less careful adversary.

The Battle of Mill Springs, also known as Fishing Creek and Logan's Crossroads, began at dawn on January 19, when advance Confederate units struck Thomas's pickets. The Union men fell back to a solid defensive line, and as Zollicoffer's brigade tried to sort itself out, Thomas hit hard on the flank. The Rebel line broke and retreated. Thomas kept after the Confederates for almost eight miles. By sundown, Crittenden's army of 4,000 men had melted away.

In punching the first hole in the Confederacy's western flank, Thomas exhibited three qualities most prized by the troops: He communicated well with them, was mindful of their safety, and he remained visible throughout the battle. The Union's high command took notice of Thomas, too, which led to one of the many disputes over rank that marred his career.

On April 6, 1862, Grant's Army of the Tennessee was ambushed by Confederates at Shiloh, on the west bank of the Tennessee River. Reinforced by Major General Don Carlos Buell's Army of the Ohio the next day, Grant managed to drive back the Confederates, but the bloody battle had cost him more than 13,000 men. Thomas's regiment arrived at Shiloh too late to do anything but provide burial details. Even though it produced a Union victory, Grant's performance at Shiloh was criticized; reporters lodged far from the battlefield spread rumors that the commander had been drunk and his men poorly prepared. Lincoln, pressured to remove Grant from command, responded: "I can't spare this man; he fights." Find out Grant's favorite brand of whiskey, Lincoln supposedly said, because "I would like to send a barrel of it to my other generals."

But General Henry Halleck pushed to reorganize his Department of the Mississippi. He promoted Thomas to major general in charge of Grant's right wing, consisting of four of Grant's divisions and one from the Army of the Ohio. Thomas asked to be relieved and sent back to his Mill Springs division. Grant resumed command of his Army of the Tennessee in June. It was a magnanimous gesture on Thomas's part, but if Grant was grateful, he never said so.

Thomas was not concerned with the trappings of high position; he wore his colonel's coat for five months after making general. He was acutely sensitive, however, to the proprieties of rank. He complained vigorously when he received a lower commission than he felt he had earned, and twice he refused to accept higher ones that he thought inappropriate.

This attention to formality was bothersome to the high command; even Lincoln got snappish about Thomas. When Buell was deemed ineffectual and replaced by William Rosecrans, Thomas's old classmate, in command of the Army of Ohio, Thomas complained he should have been next in line. Lincoln responded by forging the date of Rosecrans's commission, giving him seniority.

Rank didn't mean much at Chickamauga, but leadership mattered.

Rosecrans, with Thomas as second-in-command, led the Army of the Cumberland into Tennessee in the summer of 1863. The campaign met with early success, with Rosecrans deftly faking Confederate General Braxton Bragg out of Chattanooga and seizing a vital stronghold in an almost bloodless battle. Rosecrans could have regrouped his forces, but instead he committed the fundamental error of mistaking withdrawal for retreat. Convinced that he had the Army of Tennessee on the run, Rosecrans plunged into Bragg's trap. Bragg struck back a dozen miles south of Chattanooga, in the valley of Chickamauga Creek. *Chickamauga* was an old Cherokee word meaning "river of death," and for two days, the river lived up to its name as both sides lost nearly a third of their men.

Bad luck turned difficulty into disaster. A Union division pulled out of the line just as James Longstreet and his Southern brigades, newly arrived from Gettysburg, charged. The Union's right flank retreated, and the troops fell back along with much of the high command. Rosecrans, a devout Roman Catholic, was seen crossing himself as he rode back to Chattanooga, where he had to be helped from his horse. Assistant Secretary of

War Charles Dana, who was on the field, wrote to Washington, "Bull Run had nothing more terrible than the rout of these veteran troops. . . . They have fought to the last man, and he is running."

But Thomas wasn't running anywhere. One reporter wrote, "One of those crises had now arrived, rare in the history of any country, where the personal character and power of an individual become of incalculable value to the general welfare."

Thomas assembled a defense line along a height called Horseshoe Ridge. It didn't matter what regiment or brigade the men were from as long as they could handle a gun. There were no speeches and no calls for greatness, just George Thomas riding quietly among the men. He told a colonel the men had to hold their position regardless of the cost, and the colonel replied, "We'll hold it, General, or we'll go to heaven from it." Many of them did, but the rest held through the day, buying Rosecrans's troops time to get to safety. Field officer (and future president) James A. Garfield, who carried the orders for retreat, told Rosecrans that Thomas was "standing like a rock." Chickamauga was a bloody defeat, but Thomas had saved the Army of the Cumberland.

Lincoln, who early on knew so little about war that he took books out of the library to study military tactics, had developed the strategic sense that comes with understanding what is really important.

The army was beaten, but it still held Chattanooga. If it could stay there, the president believed, "the Rebellion must dwindle and die."

First, Rosecrans had to go. In Lincoln's harsh but accurate evaluation, after Chickamauga he was "confused and stunned like a duck hit on the head." Lincoln gave Thomas command of the Army of the Cumberland with orders to hold Chattanooga until Grant arrived to rescue the Tennessee campaign.

Grant, wet and hungry after a long ride in the rain, got to Thomas's headquarters at 9:00 p.m. Thomas was preoccupied and failed to notice that Grant was sitting by the fire with water dripping from his uniform. A member of Grant's staff had to ask before Thomas offered his commander quarters, fresh clothing, and food. The incident did nothing to improve relations between the two.

Grant largely ignored Thomas in planning the battle to regain the initiative at Chattanooga. He also wrote off the Army of the Cumberland as an attacking force, convinced that it had been used up at Chickamauga. He wanted General William Tecumseh Sherman.

Missionary Ridge, a 600-foot escarpment defended by rifle pits at the bottom and Braxton Bragg's marksmen with sixty pieces of artillery at the top, confronted the Union army at Chattanooga. Grant had in mind something grand: a massive double end run around the ridge. Sherman would swing wide to the left and deliver the main attack on Bragg's flank at dawn, while "Fighting Joe" Hooker's divisions swept in from the right to cut off the Rebel retreat. Thomas and his weary Cumberland Army, positioned in the center at the base of Missionary Ridge, were not to move until Hooker was in sight.

Grant's plan went awry almost at once. On November 23, Thomas's troops occupied Orchard Knob, high ground before Missionary Ridge; the next day, Hooker's men drove the Confederate defenders from Lookout Mountain. But the main battle had to be delayed a day so Sherman could get his men in place to assault the Confederate position at Tunnel Hill. Sherman moved at sunrise but, even outnumbering his opponents almost six to one, could make no headway. By 3:00 p.m., Sherman was still bogged down, and Hooker, who had lost five hours repairing a bridge, was nowhere to be seen.

From his command post at Orchard Knob, Grant could see the battle was getting away from him. "We must do something for Sherman," he said. Hoping a demonstration at the center would make Bragg draw troops away from Tunnel Hill, he ordered Thomas to advance on the rifle pits at the base of Missionary Ridge. The first part was easy; the Rebel riflemen retreated. But once the Cumberland men got to the pits, they were on their own, with no fire support from the rear, and they were being torn apart by short-range artillery and musket fire from the summit. They had no orders to advance or to retreat, but they wouldn't last long if they stayed put; so 18,000 men of the Army of the Cumberland charged ahead into the gunfire.

Grant watched, astonished, as the men scrambled up the slope "like a swarm of bees." He asked Thomas who had ordered the charge. Thomas said he didn't know; Gordon Granger, commander of the IV Corps, chimed in that "when those fellows get started, all hell can't stop them."

Whether an accident or a miracle - and it was called both - the charge was a blow that the Army of Tennessee could not survive. Bragg lost control of his men as they poured off the field in panic. By the time Hooker played his part in Grant's plan, sweeping in on the right flank, there was no interdicting the Southern retreat. The Union army didn't own horses that fast.

Grant was hailed as the hero of the West. The battle had not gone according to plan, but he had remained calm and altered his tactics to suit changing conditions. That was good enough for Lincoln, who summoned Grant to Washington to take overall command of the Union army. Grant was free to choose his successor in the West.

Grant kept Thomas as commander of the Army

of the Cumberland, and gave the top assignment to Sherman, whose record up until then had been uneven. Two years before, Sherman had been removed from the field under suspicion of being insane. Grant had been surprised at Shiloh largely because Sherman had not put out a proper picket line, and Sherman had failed utterly at Chattanooga. But Grant had liked the fiery redhead since Paducah, when Sherman, then senior to Grant, offered to waive any consideration of rank to keep Grant supplied. Grant was putting together a new command structure, and he knew he could work with Sherman. He wasn't so sure about Thomas.

Thomas and Sherman were opposites. While Thomas took to his bunk, Sherman prowled the camp at night in his undershirt, smoking cigars. Thomas measured his words; Sherman freely expressed an opinion on everything. But each was a superb commander. Thomas was a craftsman who put every element in place; Sherman was an artist, sloppy about details, who dealt in visions. They complemented each other. Sherman said of Thomas: "He's my off-wheel horse and knows how to pull with me, though he doesn't pull in the same way."

In the spring of 1864, there was some friction between the two as they marched their troops through Georgia toward Atlanta. Many of Thomas's 60,000 Cumberland soldiers complained that they did the fighting while Sherman got the glory. Sherman believed in moving fast and traveling light; he hated baggage trains and ordered them kept as small as possible. Thomas, who had wrenched his back in a train accident before the war, liked to take care of himself and his staff. Sherman liked to ride up to the Cumberland Army camp as if he had come upon a construction site in the Georgia countryside and ask a sentry what it was. When told it was General Thomas's command, Sherman replied, "Oh, yes, Thomastown. A very pretty place indeed. It appears to be growing rapidly."

Mistakes were made that might have been avoided with more trust. Sherman missed a chance at Resaca to deploy Thomas's heavy striking force to block the withdrawal of Joseph Johnston's Tennessee army. Against Thomas's advice, Sherman ordered up a bloody and needless battle at Kenesaw Mountain, in which Thomas lost more than 1,900 men trying to storm a position that was taken easily by maneuver a few days later.

Nevertheless, the Georgia campaign was a success. On July 22, 1864, Sherman and Thomas clashed with the Army of Tennessee, under John B. Hood, at Atlanta in a battle that killed Union General James B. McPherson. The city fell on September 2 after Union forces captured the railroad and cut off supply lines, forcing Hood's men to retreat. In the North, the capture of Atlanta was hailed as a decisive blow to the Confederacy – and not incidentally, the victory that sealed Lincoln's re-election. Morale was high in the Union army. The question was how to end the campaign.

Sherman's orders were to pursue the Army of Tennessee, but the commander instead proposed a march to the sea. "If we can march a well appointed army right through this territory," he wrote Grant, "it is a demonstration to the world foreign and domestic, that we have a power which [Jefferson] Davis can not resist. This is not war, but rather statesmanship." It would also further ruin the South, since the army would "live off the land," with foragers known as bummers confiscating food and supplies for the troops and plundering factories, rail facilities, and farms that might prolong Southern resistance. Grant didn't like the idea at first but acquiesced when Sherman promised both to sweep to the Atlantic shore and to have Thomas pursue Hood's Tennesseans.

Sherman's decision to split forces was brilliant in that it allowed both generals to do what they did best. Sherman could speed up his march to the sea while Thomas could attack John Hood.

Thomas and Hood met on the frozen turf outside Nashville. Hood's battered 30,000-man army was no match for Thomas's 55,000 invigorated Union men. But Hood was a gambler and decided to trust to what Albert Sidney Johnston had called "the iron dice of battle." He ordered his army to charge Thomas head-on.

"I don't like the looks of this fight," said Confederate General Benjamin Franklin Cheatham, a veteran of the Mexican War who had fought at Belmont, Shiloh, Perryville, Stones River, Chickamauga, and Chattanooga. Cheatham had seen more combat than most men, but he had never seen anything like the afternoon of November 30, 1864, when the Army of Tennessee threw itself on the Union lines at Franklin. It looked at first as if the Rebels might win. They ripped into the Union outer defenses, scattering two brigades and capturing eight guns. But in a textbook demonstration of how to commit reserves, Union brigade commander Emerson Opdycke plugged the gap in a melee of hand-to-hand fighting. Hood kept at it for almost six hours, finally calling off the attack at 9:00 p.m.

Thomas retired to Nashville. Grant, in his Virginia headquarters, was afraid Hood might get loose and badgered Thomas to attack. But Thomas stalled. The weather was too bad, he said, and the ground had iced over, making attack difficult. Besides, there were horses to look after and men to equip before fighting again. "I thought," Thomas said, "after what I had done in the war, that I ought to be trusted to decide when the battle should be fought. I thought I knew better when it should be fought than anyone could know as far off as City Point, Virginia."

Thomas continued his careful preparations while his superiors fumed. Sherman wrote to Grant on December 16: "I know full well that General Thomas is slow in mind and in action but he is judicious and brave, and the troops feel great confidence in him. I still hope he will out-maneuver and destroy Hood." On the day Sherman wrote, destroying Hood was precisely what Thomas was doing.

Grant and Thomas had different ideas about what was important. Grant was thinking about his final campaign to defeat the Confederacy; Thomas, he believed, was putting the campaign at risk by fussing over details. Thomas had a more immediate goal in mind; he saw no virtue in a partial victory and would continue the fight only when certain he could finish it.

Grant became so upset that, in six days, he scribbled out three separate orders relieving Thomas. Deciding to take command himself, he gave the last order to a telegraph operator and went to his hotel. The operator decided to delay sending the telegram until he received the regular night traffic from Nashville. The wires started clacking at 11:00 p.m.; by the time the code clerks deciphered the messages, it was over. Thomas had struck Nashville on December 15, smashing one corps and, the next day, two more. The Army of Tennessee had ceased to exist.

Sherman, fresh from his capture of Savannah, sent Thomas a self-congratulatory Christmas Day message that "had any misfortune befallen you I should have reproached myself for taking away so large a proportion of the army and leaving you too weak to cope with Hood. But as the events have turned out my judgment has been sustained."

Grant thought Thomas's pursuit of Hood inadequate, despite the fact there wasn't much left of the Army of Tennessee to pursue. After Thomas retired to winter quarters, Grant split up the Army of the Cumberland and doled it out to other units until it was essentially reduced to the IV Corps. Thomas's career as an army commander was over.

Edwin M. Stanton approached Grant about rewarding Thomas with the three stars of a major general. Grant started to block the promotion but later relented. On Christmas Day, Thomas's name was on a promotions list headed to the Senate for confirmation. He was ranked behind Sherman, George Meade, and Philip Sheridan. His unit surgeon, George Cooper, looked at the slate and remarked, "better late than never."

"It is too late to be appreciated," Thomas replied. "I earned this at Chickamauga." Then he started to cry.

In May 1865, after Lee and Johnston had sent their men home, the Union army staged a parade. On the day given to Sherman and his armies of the

West, George Thomas watched from the reviewing stand. As units of the old Army of the Cumberland rolled by in their insolent western gait, Thomas whispered to no one in particular, "They made me."

After the war, Thomas briefly was caught up in the turbulent politics of the Reconstruction. Andrew Johnson tried to exploit Thomas by offering to make him commanding general in place of Grant. Thomas refused, saying the promotion was too late a reward for his war service and not justified by anything he had done since.

Thomas was assigned in 1869 to command the Division of the Pacific, with headquarters in San Francisco. Concerned with details to the last, he sat at his desk on March 28, 1870, to write a letter to a newspaper correcting an article concerning his handling of the Nashville campaign. Several pages into the letter, he was writing, "this was a very brilliant battle, most disastrous to the enemy, and as the writer in the *Tribune* says, no doubt contributed materially to the crowning success at Nashville. . . ." Suddenly, the bold penmanship quavered. Thomas suffered a stroke and collapsed. He died that evening.

12
LINCOLN'S PLAN FOR RECONSTRUCTION
– R. N. CURRENT

In his annual message to Congress in December 1863, with the Confederacy tottering toward defeat in the Civil War, Abraham Lincoln looked ahead to postwar reconstruction.

Anyone who knew Lincoln would have known his design for a restored Union would not be hateful and vindictive. It would not rule out the very spirit of reunion. His view had never been narrowly sectional. Though he was against slavery and secession, he was never anti-Southern. But his moderation was to put him at loggerheads with the radical faction of his own Republican party – men who were all-out abolitionists, who despised the South.

He had said in his first inaugural: "Physically we cannot separate," and he often returned to this theme. To "separate our common country into two nations" was intolerable. The indispensable Union was Lincoln's key consideration in reconstruction, but not the only factor.

Loyalty was important to Lincoln, but so was trust. In considering the formation of the new state of West Virginia – a Union stronghold carved from the Rebel state, Virginia – the president expressed his view that only those loyal to the United States could be regarded as competent voters. He repudiated the policy of New York Representative Fernando Wood, which would accept Southerners in Congress before resistance was ended, and loyalty assured. On the other side, he disallowed the importing of Northern politicians to hold office in Southern states, a policy that became known as carpetbagging. Union officers who were not citizens of a captured Southern state, he ruled, should not seek election to represent it in Congress "at the point of a bayonet."

Reconstruction, Lincoln knew, would have to be accomplished in stages; the plan he put forth on December 8, 1863, was only the first step. It set the terms and conditions for pardon, and for restoring a Southern state to the Union.

The offer of pardon (with stated exceptions) and restoration of rights (except as to slaves) was held out to anyone in a seceded state who swore an oath to support the Constitution of the United States "and the union of the States thereunder." The oath-taker also must swear to abide by all acts of Congress and presidential proclamations relating to slaves unless repealed, modified, or declared void by the Supreme Court.

A state's reentry into the Union was more complicated. For a state government to be recognized as valid, it had to be elected by a number not less than one-tenth of those voting in 1860. Lincoln was putting the formation of any new state government in the hands of the people of the state – not any self-appointed power-grabbers, and not the federal government.

Lincoln's job was to reassemble the shattered pieces of a disrupted social and political order, in the midst of war. He was willing to accept informality and makeshift solutions. He would not throw away the cause while futilely waiting for perfection.

The reconstruction was to start immediately. Some captured Southern states could be rebuilt and restored even during the war - indeed as an important factor in waging and ending the war. Lincoln hoped to set an example of cooperation for other Southerners as armies advanced and national authority was extended. In time of war, he thought, prepare for peace.

The response to Lincoln's plan was mixed. The Washington *Chronicle* praised the announcement, noting that it was delivered from a point of strength. The Union's armies were victorious, its navy in control of Southern coasts, and its cause strengthened by increased friendship of foreign nations. Lincoln's offer of pardon was evidence of his kindness and sympathy toward the people of the South, the newspaper's editor stated.

The day before Lincoln's proclamation, Jefferson Davis issued his own. Both statements targeted peace, but Davis's tone was more combative. After a depressing account of Confederate military reverses, the Southern president denounced the "barbarous policy" and "savage ferocity" of "our enemies." The Northerners, "hardened by crime," refused "even to listen to proposals . . . of recognizing the impassable gulf which divides us," Davis told his Congress.

It was obvious from the start that Lincoln's plan would not go smoothly, but steps were taken on several fronts to make it known and put it into operation. Army officers handed out copies of the proclamation to the soldiers. During raids into enemy territory, troops were detailed "for the purpose of distributing the proclamation broadcast among rebel soldiers and people, and in the highways and byways." Aid and protection were to be extended to all who declared loyalty.

District attorneys throughout the country were instructed that the "President's pardon of a person guilty of ... rebellion ... [would] relieve that person for the penalties" of that crime. Federal court proceedings were to be ceased if the accused swore loyalty to the United States. This rule did not apply to men in custody or on parole as prisoners of war, whose only option was to apply to the president for clemency. But it did apply to persons still at large who agreed to surrender.

Lincoln saw Louisiana as an early opportunity to make reconstruction a reality. The Union had occupied New Orleans – the largest Confederate city - since May 1, 1862. The first phase was army rule under General Benjamin Franklin Butler, a tough but effective commander. Local politicians who cooperated with Butler had a good chance of being retained; all others were dismissed. Within a month, New Orleans's mayor was deposed and imprisoned, and George F. Shepley, acting closely with Butler, took over. In June, Shepley became military governor of Louisiana; soon afterward, he had the rank of brigadier general. It was a bad start to Lincoln's reconstruction.

The women of New Orleans had made a game of harassing the occupying Union troops, insulting the men and emptying chamber pots on their heads from second-story windows. Butler issued an order that the troops could treat any such woman as if she were a prostitute – a measure that quickly ended the harassment game but made the name of "Beast Butler" a hated byword in the South and hampered postwar reconciliation. Many were relieved when President Lincoln removed Butler from his Louisiana command on December 16, 1862. His successor, as commander of the military forces stationed in Louisiana and Texas, was Major General Nathaniel P. Banks.

A former congressman and governor of Massachusetts, Banks was more moderate and in line with Lincoln's policy than Butler. Some, including Secretary of the Navy Gideon Welles, resented Banks. He was not a West Point man but had impressed Lincoln enough with his organization of the Massachusetts militia to be given command of troops charged with suppressing secessionist thoughts in slave-holding Maryland.

Complicating matters for Banks, Shepley stayed on as military governor of Louisiana, and like Butler, he was an obstacle to reconstruction. The conflict carried over into Congress, which after a bitter election battle in December 1862 had seated as Louisiana representatives the radical B. F. Flanders and moderate Michael Hahn, a citizen of Louisiana. A period of bickering followed as these two factions sought to control the state-making process.

Governor Shepley proceeded to make a registry of voters, appointing another radical, T. J. Durant, as commissioner of registration. In the summer of 1863, still months before Lincoln's proclamation, Durant required Louisianans to swear allegiance to the Union before they could be registered as voters. It was Durant's idea that ten loyal men in a parish, if no more could be registered, would be a sufficient basis for an election. Lincoln approved the registration and wanted it pushed.

Lincoln was trying to avoid seeming to dictate; he wanted to let the Louisiana political process work itself out. But jurisdictional disputes soon forced him to intervene. Shepley and Durant claimed they were exclusively charged with the work of reconstruction in Louisiana, and Banks had not felt authorized to interfere with them. Banks wrote to Lincoln on December 16, 1863, that he was only in partial command. "There are not less than four distinct governments here," he wrote, "claiming . . . independent powers based upon instructions received directly from Washington, and recognizing no other authority than their own."

Lincoln had supposed all the time that Banks was in command but had not made that point sufficiently clear. In a strongly worded reply, he stressed to Banks: You are master. Shepley, he wrote, was to "assist" Banks, not to "thwart" him. He restated Banks's objective: "Give us a free State reorganization of Louisiana in the shortest possible time."

In January and February 1864, Banks issued proclamations for two kinds of elections: an election for governor under the Louisiana constitution of 1853, and an election of delegates to a convention to make a new state constitution. Banks declared that elected officials could be removed if they attempted to change federal statutes regarding slavery. Recognition of the end of slavery in Louisiana was causing less difficulty than expected. While the planter class wanted to keep the institution, they were in the minority; most of the people were ready to accept emancipation.

Lincoln told Banks to proceed "with all possible dispatch . . . Frame orders, and fix times and places for this and that. . . ."

Both elections were a success. On February 22, 1864, 54 percent of the 11,411 total voters chose the moderate Michael Hahn to govern the newly formed Louisiana. The rest of the votes were split almost evenly between the radical Flanders and J. Q. A. Fellows, nominated by pro-slavery conservatives. On March 28, 1864, the delegates were chosen to draft a new constitution. They were not a distinguished group but represented the people rather than politicians.

The constitutional convention labored from April to July. The delegates voted seventy to sixteen to abolish slavery. Black suffrage, a new and difficult question, was a more difficult issue to resolve. After voting it down, the convention reconsidered; it then empowered the legislature to grant blacks the right to vote. The constitution also required that a militia be enrolled without distinction of color.

On September 5, 1864, the people of Louisiana voted 6,836 to 1,566 to ratify the constitution. Members of Congress were chosen by popular election, after which the legislature selected two senators. Lincoln's work was done; it was now up to Congress to complete the reformation of Louisiana by validating the state elections. But that wasn't easy.

Louisiana radicals rejected the new constitution and proceeded to make their influence felt in Congress, where they had the support of many Lincoln opponents. As Lincoln had hoped, the Louisiana movement had served as the model for other captured Southern states. Tennessee, where Andrew Johnson had been appointed military governor in March 1862, and Arkansas, which came under Union control in September 1863, adopted constitutions identical to Louisiana's. But in December 1864, Congress refused to count any of the votes from Louisiana, Arkansas, and Tennessee. As a result, the states' elected representatives were denied their seats in Washington.

The Congressional majority sided with the radicals, who wanted more complete change in the South. They did not accept Lincoln's standard of 10-percent loyalty, insisting that a majority of a state's electorate must swear allegiance to the Union before the state could be readmitted. Leading this charge were Ohio Senator Benjamin F. Wade and Henry Winter Davis, the representative from Maryland.

Davis had made himself chairman of a special House committee to study alternatives to the president's reconstruction plan. In February 1864, he sponsored a bill that guaranteed "usurped or overthrown" Southern states a republican form of government. But in a preamble to the bill, Davis implied these states were no longer in the Union: They were entitled neither to be represented in Congress nor to take any part in the national government.

The measure of a state's loyalty mattered most. Davis's bill required a majority of white male citizens to take the oath to start the remaking of a state government. Also, that majority could include only men who had never voluntarily borne arms against the United States, aided in arming forces hostile to the Union, or supported any "pretended government." The bill also barred any former officeholder under a "usurping power" to vote or hold office in the recreated state.

On May 4, the House passed the bill along party lines. Extreme though it was, the bill did not go far enough to suit all the radicals who voted for it. Thaddeus Stevens, representing Pennsylvania, advocated a provision that let the federal government claim all Confederate-owned land parcels of 100 acres or more.

Wade took charge of the bill in the Senate, where he tried unsuccessfully to strike the word "white" from the oath requirement. Other senators succeeded in attaching amendments, none of them drastic, and the minor differences between the House and Senate versions had to be reconciled by a conference committee. The Senate finally passed the Wade-Davis bill on July 4, 1864, within an hour of the session's expiration.

Unless the president signed the bill within ten days, it would fail to become law by a process called pocket veto. Lincoln could have let the ten days pass in silence; instead, he chose the unusual course of issuing a proclamation. He announced on July 8 that he was "unprepared, by a formal approval of this bill, to be inflexibly committed to any single plan of restoration," and that he was "also unprepared to declare that the free-state constitutions and governments already adopted and installed in Arkansas and Louisiana" should be "set aside and held for nought."

Lincoln wanted to fight for his vision of reconstruction, but he had lost political strength as the Union army failed repeatedly to capitalize on Confederate weakness and end the war. The long

Congressional recess would hamstring legislative action until after the 1864 presidential election; his statement was meant to frame the debate on his own terms.

Lincoln's biggest problem with the bill was its fundamental assertion that Southern states had to be reinstated into the Union. In his view, the secession of these states was never constitutionally valid, and they were still a part of the Union, although there were conditions for full participation in the government. The president disagreed with the assessment of loyalty as a matter of past conduct, not of present attitude or future promise. "On principle I dislike an oath which requires a man to swear he *has* not done wrong," Lincoln said. "It rejects the Christian principle of forgiveness on terms of repentance. I think it is enough if the man does no wrong hereafter."

Lincoln also believed the bill would block the reconstruction efforts already underway in Louisiana, Tennessee, and Arkansas. He let the bill die but announced that he was ready to give executive aid to the people of any state who chose to adopt either his or the Wade-Davis plan for reconstruction.

"What an infamous proclamation!" Thad Stevens wrote a friend. "The idea of pocketing a bill and then issuing a proclamation as to how far he will conform to it. . . ." Though Lincoln had intended to mollify the radicals, he had succeeded only in exasperating them. Stevens asked, then answered his own question: "What are we to do? Condemn privately and applaud publicly!"

On August 4, Wade and Davis published a manifesto in the *New York Tribune* denouncing Lincoln for proceeding with his reconstruction plan. They charged the president with "grave Executive usurpation" and the perpetration of a "studied outrage on the legislative authority." They condemned his "shadows of governments" in Arkansas and Louisiana as "mere oligarchies . . . (and) creatures of his will."

The manifesto insinuated that Lincoln's purpose in hastening the readmission of Southern states was to create additional electoral votes and assure his own re-election. It included the not-so-veiled threat that Lincoln's "rash and fatal act" had been "a blow at the friends of his Administration . . . the rights of humanity . . . and the principles of Republican government." The president "must understand that our support is of a cause and not of a man," Wade and Davis wrote, and "if he wishes our support, [he must] confine himself to his Executive duties . . . and leave political reorganization to Congress."

Some conservative Republicans came to Lincoln's defense. *The New York Times*, edited by Lincoln campaign manager Henry J. Raymond, deplored the "ultra radicalism and barbarism" of Wade and

Davis, whom the newspaper called dangerous revolutionaries. "They have sustained the war not as a means of restoring the Union, but to free the slaves, seize the lands, crush the spirit, destroy the rights and blot out forever the political freedom of the people inhabiting the Southern States."

Lincoln's Cabinet members were alarmed by the protest. Welles assumed Wade was motivated by presidential aspirations of his own. Secretary of the Interior J. P. Usher argued that Lincoln had tried to "oblige this class of men," and had given them little "cause & reason to assail him," but they would never be satisfied. Montgomery Blair, the postmaster general, saw them as enemies of the Union and the administration, which had to face Jefferson Davis, Robert E. Lee, and the rebels on one side, and "Henry Winter Davis & Ben Wade and all such hell cats on the other."

Lincoln wondered aloud to William Seward "whether these men intended openly to oppose my election," and commented to journalist Noah Brooks: "To be wounded in the house of one's friends is perhaps the most grievous affliction that can befall a man."

The president's suspicion was correct: Davis and Wade's protest signaled a movement to replace Lincoln as the Republican candidate in mid-campaign. Davis soon circulated among prominent party members a petition for a new national "Union" or "People's" convention to meet in September and nominate another candidate who could "save the country from anarchy and rebellion."

A secret council met August 14 in New York. The members included *New York Tribune* editor Horace Greeley, New York Mayor George Opdyke, attorney David Dudley Field, and John Austin Stevens, president of the New York Bank of Commerce and treasurer of the Union National Committee. The group grew in number and respectability. In August 1864, while the war was still swinging back toward the Confederacy, the conspirators were buoyed by the seeming hopelessness of Lincoln's chances for re-election in the fall.

Davis was said to favor Charles Francis Adams, the Massachusetts representative and son of former President John Quincy Adams as a candidate. But most of the others preferred a military man like General Grant, William Tecumseh Sherman, "the Superb" Winfield Scott Hancock, or "Beast Butler." Grant endorsed Lincoln and refused to be made a rallying point for opposition to his commander-in-chief.

The leaders of the anti-Lincoln movement disagreed on tactics as well as personnel. Some wanted a new candidate; others were willing to proceed only if Lincoln could be induced to resign as the party's candidate.

Lincoln knew about the movement against him, as well as the consensus among political experts that his chances of re-election were slim. But he refused to make concessions to his opponents, on either side. On August 23, Lincoln wrote a memorandum which he folded, pasted, and gave to his Cabinet members to endorse, sight unseen. "This morning, as for some days past, it seems exceedingly probable that this Administration will not be re-elected," he wrote. "Then it will be my duty to so co-operate with the President elect, as to save the Union between the election and the inauguration; as he will have secured his election on such ground that he can not possibly save it afterwards."

This, Lincoln recalled after the election, was at a time "when as yet we had no adversary, and seemed to have no friends." The Democratic convention was six days away. Lincoln had not abandoned all hope. He had been heard saying that he knew he would be "badly beaten . . . unless some great change (occurred in the military situation)."

The pre-convention favorite for the Democratic nomination was erstwhile Army of the Potomac commander George B. McClellan. War Democrats believed only McClellan could rally the soldier vote in the field and at home against Lincoln. Republicans thought McClellan could win, too. McClellan, though, was not sure he would run. "It is very doubtful whether anything would now induce me to consent to have my name used," he wrote as late as June 25.

Lincoln loyalists thought they would be doing the president a favor by convincing McClellan to sit out the election. In July, Francis P. Blair, father of Lincoln's postmaster general, visited McClellan in New York with a proposition: The general would be restored to command if he would disavow any presidential aspirations. McClellan was noncommittal. Blair returned to Washington to report to Lincoln, who, hearing of the plan for the first time, offered no comment. Nothing came of it, except for some campaign propaganda later on.

McClellan still led all contenders when the Democrats convened on August 29 in Chicago. The delegates took only two days to nominate McClellan for president and Ohio Representative George H. Pendleton for vice president. Pendleton's selection complicated matters; Gentleman George, as he was known, was a Peace Democrat, and McClellan was a War Democrat. The party was counting on McClellan's war record to win the soldier vote, but also hoping to capitalize on anti-war sentiment with a peace platform. Republicans seized on the contradiction.

The question that needled McClellan was which should come first: union or peace. Many in his party sought armistice without stipulations, trusting that reunion would follow. The other faction demanded that reunion be made a precondition of any cease-fire agreement. For days, men of both groups pelted McClellan with contradictory advice.

Meanwhile, Lincoln finally achieved the "great change" he had longed for in the war. On September 2, Western troops from Sherman's Army of the Tennessee had pushed into Georgia and captured Atlanta. The victory would be sealed by Sherman's devastating March to the Sea and north through the Carolinas, but it was seen immediately as a decisive blow to the Confederacy, and many wavering votes swung to Lincoln's re-election.

McClellan was still hovering between union and peace as he drafted a letter announcing his candidacy. In the fourth version, dated September 8, he came out for union as the prerequisite of peace.

The publication of his letter provoked new disagreements within his party. Some of the peace men wanted to repudiate McClellan and reassemble the convention to nominate a new candidate. But most agreed that McClellan could win even after the victory at Atlanta. The radical Republicans had declared the war a failure, to be blamed on the Lincoln Administration; as long as the voters saw it that way, they would seek change. In a time long before opinion polling, the shift in the national mood went unperceived.

That a presidential election was being held at all was miraculous. In the midst of a civil war, the American people were about to assess their leadership and perhaps change their rulers by the same orderly processes as in times of peace. "If we come triumphantly out of this war, with a presidential election in the midst of it," political philosopher Francis Lieber wrote to Massachusetts Senator Charles Summer, a radical Republican, at the end of August, 1864, ". . . I shall call it the greatest miracle in all the historic course of events."

September elections for state officers in Maine and Vermont had overwhelmingly favored Republicans. On October 10, Ohio voters seated seventeen Republicans in the U.S. House of Representatives – an increase of twelve. The next night, President Lincoln anxiously watched the election returns from Indiana and Pennsylvania. At 8:00 p.m., he went to the telegraph office in the War Department. The place was locked, and Stanton had taken the keys upstairs, but "a shivering messenger was pacing to and fro in the moonlight over the withered leaves," and he let the president and his party in at a side door.

When there was a lull in the dispatches coming in over the wires, Lincoln - as he often did in worried moments - took a volume of Petroleum V. Nasby, a pseudonym for political commentator David Ross Locke, from his pocket and read several chapters aloud. The early returns from Indiana were encouraging, but those from Pennsylvania less so. The final count, settled a few days later, showed Republicans gaining four seats in Indiana and three in Pennsylvania.

Lincoln was not overconfident about his own chances in November. On October 13, again at the War Department's telegraph office, he jotted down his estimate of the electoral vote. In the Democratic column, he tallied 114 votes from New York, Pennsylvania, New Jersey, Delaware, Maryland, Missouri, Kentucky, and Illinois. In the Republican column, the other states added up to 117 electoral votes. Lincoln concluded he would win by a narrow margin. Even if this majority had been certain, he would not have been happy with it. He wanted a decisive vindication of his party and his administration, and three votes was not enough.

In some parts of the country, the Republicans, expecting violence, awaited Election Day with apprehension. In Illinois, Stanton heard, more than 5,000 armed Confederates roamed the streets to intimidate and block Lincoln supporters from the polls.

When November 8 arrived, however, no serious disturbances interfered with polling. In Illinois, qualified voters - white men over twenty-one with a year's residence in the state - patiently waited to vote, standing single-file in long lines. Saloons were closed, and in Springfield, where it rained steadily most of the day, the *Illinois State Journal* noted that "fewer drunken people were seen upon the streets than usual." From New York, Butler, in command of the Union troops, telegraphed laconically to the War Department at noon: "The quietest city ever seen."

Washington was even quieter. The day was dark and rainy, and the city was depopulated by the homeward exodus of more than 18,000 men, mostly government employees, to cast their votes. "The rush to the cars of those going home to vote was too much for the railroads," a news dispatch reported two days before the election.

On election night, Lincoln went again to the telegraph office to get the returns. "We splashed through the grounds to the side door of the War Department," he later wrote, "where a soaked and smoking sentinel was standing in his own vapor with his huddled-up frame covered with a rubber cloak." Early returns were favorable. By midnight, Lincoln was "tolerably certain" that Maryland, Pennsylvania, most of the Middle West, and all of New England would go for him. There were no returns yet from Illinois or Iowa.

A late supper was brought in, and "the President went awkwardly and hospitably to work shovelling out the fried oysters," observed Lincoln's private secretary John Hay. As he was congratulated on what seemed a sure and decisive victory, Lincoln appeared calm. He did say "he was glad to be relieved of all suspense," Hay recalled, "and . . . grateful that the verdict of the people was likely to be so full, clear, and unmistakable that there could be no dispute."

About 2:00 a.m., a messenger brought word that a crowd of Pennsylvanians were serenading the White House. Lincoln went home, and in response to cries for a speech, spoke for a few moments. "If I know my heart, my gratitude is free from any taint of personal triumph," he concluded. "I do not impugn the motives of anyone opposed to me. It is no pleasure to me to triumph over any one, but I give thanks to the Almighty for this evidence of the people's resolution to stand by free government and the rights of humanity."

Sherman had completed his March to the Sea, and General George Henry Thomas had swept up the tattered remnants of the Southern army. Grant's forces were besieging Petersburg and driving again toward Richmond. Victory could not be deferred for long, most Northerners believed. "The people seem to have settled since the election into perfect confidence," a Washington visitor wrote in mid-February, "that the end is sure, that the South must submit and come back, that slavery is dead, & that Grant & Sherman & Thomas are masters of the situation & guarantors of their security."

As they looked hopefully ahead to a Confederate collapse, many began to think about the kind of peace that should be made, and the procedure for doing so. While Lincoln had been re-elected, the radical strength in Congress had also increased. In his State of the Union address on December 6, 1864, Lincoln declared his position: "I mean simply to say that the war will cease on the part of the government, whenever it shall have ceased on the part of those who began it." The people of the South, he said, "can, at any moment, have peace simply by laying down their arms and submitting to the national authority under the Constitution."

The president ruled out a peace mission to Richmond. "On careful consideration of all the evidence accessible it seems to me that no attempt at negotiation with the insurgent leader could result in any good," he said. "He would accept nothing short of severance of the Union - precisely what we will not and cannot give." On the topic of slavery, Lincoln repeated his declaration that "while I remain in my present position I shall not attempt to retract or modify the Emancipation Proclamation, nor shall I return to slavery any person who is free by the terms of that proclamation, or by any of the Acts of Congress."

The 38th Congress had met for the last time on March 4, 1865; the 39th would not convene until December unless the president called it into special session. Lincoln began his second term, which was not expected to be his last; gamblers were betting he would be re-elected again in 1868. After four years as a war president, he was looking ahead to four more as a peace president.

Inauguration day dawned dark, and rain fell steadily throughout the morning. The streets of Washington, especially Pennsylvania Avenue, were filled with mud. The rain ceased before the ceremonies began, but most spectators, standing in front of the east entrance of the Capitol, already were thoroughly bedraggled.

The ceremonies were poorly planned, according to Welles, who wrote: "All was confusion and without order - a jumble." Many who heard Vice President Andrew Johnson's rambling and maudlin inauguration speech wondered whether he was drunk. In fact, he was ill. Strongly urged by Lincoln to be present, Johnson had fortified himself with whiskey beforehand.

Lincoln's inaugural address was short – 703 words that, including pauses for applause, took less than seven minutes to deliver. So many public declarations had been made during the war, Lincoln remarked, that "little that is new could be presented." Still, the speech is regarded by many as one of Lincoln's greatest; it is inscribed, along with his Gettysburg Address, in the Lincoln Memorial.

He reminded the American people ". . . four years ago all thoughts were anxiously directed to an impending civil war. All dreaded it, all sought to avert it. . . . Both parties deprecated war; but one of them would *make* war rather than let the nation survive; and the other would *accept* war rather than let it perish. And the war came."

Then he elaborated upon the basic issue: the "peculiar and powerful interest" of slavery. "All knew that this interest was, somehow, the cause of the war," Lincoln said.

Lincoln concluded with the lines that made the address forever memorable: "With malice toward none; with charity for all; with firmness in the right, as God gives us to see the right, let us strive on to finish the work we are in; to bind up the nation's wounds; to care for him who shall have borne the battle, and for his widow, and his orphan - to do all which may achieve and cherish a just, and a lasting peace, among ourselves, and with all nations."

After reaching a furious pitch in the summer of 1864, the debate over reconstruction had been toned down during the final weeks of the presidential campaign. When Lee's surrender brought the issue to the forefront again, Lincoln and the radicals were even further apart than before. In early April 1865, Lincoln seemed willing to readmit the Southern states on even more generous terms than he had announced in December 1863. The radicals demanded terms even more rigorous than those embodied in the Wade-Davis bill, which Lincoln had refused to sign.

On April 10, in Washington, Benjamin Butler called for the leaders of the rebellion to be disfranchised and disqualified for public office; and the masses, including blacks, to be granted immediately all rights of citizenship. The next evening, in Baltimore on court duty, Chief Justice Salmon P. Chase dined with Henry Winter Davis and other Maryland radicals, then wrote a letter to Lincoln. "It will be, hereafter, counted equally a crime and a folly," Chase wrote, "if the colored loyalists of the rebel states shall be left to the control of restored rebels, not likely, in that case, to be either wise or just, until taught both wisdom and justice by new calamities."

On April 11, Lincoln made his own, last contribution to the public debate when he addressed a crowd on the White House grounds. After a few congratulatory words on Grant's victory over Lee at Appomattox, he defended at some length his own reconstruction view.

The problem, as Lincoln saw it, was essentially one of re-establishing the national authority throughout the South. It was complicated by the fact that there was "no authorized organ" in the South to deal with. "Nor is it a small additional embarrassment that we, the loyal people, differ among ourselves as to the mode, manner, and means of reconstruction," he said.

The president said he had been criticized because he did not seem to have a fixed opinion on whether the seceded States were "in the Union or out of it." He dismissed that question as "a merely pernicious abstraction" and declared: "We all agree that the seceded States, so called, are out of their proper practical relation with the Union; and that the sole object of the government, civil and military, in regard to those States is to again get them into that proper practical relation."

He had been criticized for establishing and sustaining the state government of Louisiana, which rested on the support of only 10 percent of voters and excluded blacks. He granted that the Louisiana government would be better supported by a larger electorate, including at least "the very intelligent" blacks and those who had served as soldiers. "Concede that the new government of Louisiana is only to what it should be as the egg is to the fowl," Lincoln said, "we shall sooner have the fowl by hatching the egg than by smashing it." The loyalists of the South would be encouraged and the blacks better off, he argued, if Louisiana were quickly readmitted to the Union. Doing so would engender support for the Thirteenth Amendment to abolish slavery.

Lincoln applied the same logic to the rest of the South, "and yet so great peculiarities pertain to each state; and such important and sudden changes occur in the same state," he said, "that no exclusive, and inflexible plan can safely be prescribed as to details and collaterals."

In conclusion, Lincoln said that it might become his duty "to make some new announcement to the people of the South. I am considering, and shall not fail to act, when satisfied that action will be proper."

The speech aroused speculation about Lincoln's intentions and provoked mixed feelings about his approach to reconstruction. The editor of the Philadelphia *Public Ledger* noted that the president had indicated his "feelings and wishes" rather than his "fixed opinions," then commended him for his lack of "passion or malignancy" toward the former rebels. The Cincinnati *Gazette*'s Washington correspondent believed Lincoln's position was accepted by all but radical Republicans, who demanded that rebel leaders be punished and the rebel states subjected to "preliminary training" before being restored to the Union. "The desire of the people for a settlement - speedy and final - upon the easiest possible terms, will, it is believed, sustain the President in his policy foreshadowed in his speech," the *Gazette* reported.

When Lincoln's Cabinet met on the morning of April 14, with General Grant present, some of his own advisers made it clear that a settlement would not be reached easily. Stanton called for military occupation as a preliminary step toward the reorganization of Southern states, and for Virginia and North Carolina to be combined in a single military district. Welles argued that merging the two would destroy the individuality of the states. Lincoln sustained Welles's objection but did not completely repudiate Stanton's plan. Instead, he suggested Stanton revise it to deal with Virginia and North Carolina separately, and asked him to provide copies of the revised plan at the next Cabinet meeting.

Before the meeting adjourned, Lincoln said he was glad Congress was not in session. It would be up to the House and Senate to accept or reject new members from the Southern states, but he believed the president had the power to recognize state governments. He could collect taxes in the South, see to it that the mail was delivered there, and appoint federal officials. He knew radicals of both parties did not agree with him, but for the moment they had no official platform from which to object. He did not intend to call a special session before December, he told Speaker of the House Schuyler Colfax as he was leaving to go to Ford's Theater. A few hours later, at 10:25 p.m. on April 14, Lincoln was watching *Our American Cousin* when John Wilkes Booth barged into the presidential box. As the audience laughed at the antics on stage, Booth shot Lincoln in the back of the head.

When Congress convened its regular session in December 1865, Andrew Johnson had been president for nearly eight months. In the days following Lincoln's assassination, Johnson spoke in radical rhetoric. He ordered the arrest of Jefferson Davis and other Confederate leaders on the charge of complicity in the assassination. But Johnson and the radicals soon disagreed on reconstruction.

That summer, Johnson succeeded in restoring state governments according to a plan requiring them to abolish slavery, retract their ordinances of secession, and repudiate their debts accumulated in the Confederate cause.

In December, the radicals in Congress refused to seat the senators and representatives from the restored states. After checking Johnson's program, the radicals proceeded to undo it while impeaching the president. Eventually, they carried through their own program of military occupation, similar to the one Stanton had proposed at the Cabinet meeting of April 14.

Whether Lincoln would have taken the same steps as Johnson is hard to say. Certainly Lincoln would not have hounded Davis or other Confederate officials. To his Cabinet in April, he had expressed his hope that there would be no persecution, no bloody work, with respect to any of the late enemy. "None need expect he would take any part in hanging or killing those men, even the worst of them," Welles paraphrased him. "Frighten them out of the country, open the gates, let down the bars, scare them off, said he, throwing up his hands as if scaring sheep."

The rest is conjecture. It seems likely that, with his superior talent for political management, Lincoln would have avoided the worst of Johnson's clashes with Congress. Yet he scarcely could have escaped the conflict itself.

13
THE BIG PARADE
– THOMAS FLEMING

W hen the Civil War sputtered out early in May 1865, politicians in Washington wondered what to do with the two massive Union armies that were near the capital. The Army of the Potomac, commanded by Major General George Gordon Meade, had won the war in the East. The Army of the Tennessee, or the Western Army, had marched through Georgia to the sea under Major General William Tecumseh Sherman.

The sheer logistics of getting vast numbers of men off the payroll was problem enough. But Sherman's Western Army was more than a problem; it was a threat. The men around the volatile Secretary of War Edwin Stanton suspected Sherman and his men of contemplating the overthrow of the federal government.

Lincoln was dead, and Andrew Johnson displayed the usual bewilderment of vice-presidents suddenly catapulted from superfluity to power. Stanton stepped into this void of leadership.

In prosecuting the band that had conspired with John Wilkes Booth to assassinate Lincoln, Stanton was trying to convict the entire South of murder by naming Jefferson Davis himself, with several other high-ranking Confederates, as defendants. The trial, conducted before a military tribunal at the Arsenal Penitentiary, was tainted by perjury and fictitious testimony. Stanton's attitude toward Sherman was not improved by Sherman's brother-in-law, the former Major General Thomas Ewing, Jr., who was defending three of Booth's co-conspirators - physician Samuel Mudd, Samuel Arnold, and Ford Theater stagehand Edman Spangler.

But Stanton's mistrust of Sherman was more directly tied to the treaty of peace he had negotiated with Confederate General Joseph Johnston. Two weeks after Appomattox, in Raleigh, Sherman had sat down with his fellow West Pointer and signed a document that endorsed the legitimacy of Southern state governments as soon as they took an oath of allegiance to the United States. It also guaranteed the ex-Rebels political rights as well as "rights of person and property."

Sherman thought he was following Lincoln's policy of reconciliation, but Stanton and other radical Republicans believed he sought to reconstitute the South, complete with slavery. The secretary of war called in reporters and accused Sherman of insubordination and treason. Headlines across the country echoed the condemnation.

Sherman's soldiers rallied behind their Uncle Billy; they burned Northern newspapers in Raleigh, and many feared they might burn newspaper offices.

Johnson, eager to change the mood in the capital, opted to hold a parade: He approved of a plan for a "grand review" of both Union armies, marching separately on successive days. It was a brilliant plan - not only did it keep the potentially clashing armies separate and defuse the political mine fizzling under the government's feet, it produced the greatest parade in American history.

The behavior of Sherman and his men as they marched toward Washington was not reassuring. Camping outside Richmond, the soldiers were annoyed to discover that General Henry Halleck had ordered them barred from the city. Tempers flared, and skirmishes erupted between the Westerners and Army of the Potomac units guarding routes into the Confederate capital.

When Halleck, second-in-command of the Union army, invited Sherman to parade one of his corps through Richmond as a symbolic gesture, Sherman told him to go to hell. Halleck, siding with Stanton, had sent telegrams to Western subordinates, such as George Thomas in Nashville, telling them to disregard all orders from Sherman. Sherman found out and, "outraged beyond measure," said only a direct order from the Union general-in-chief, Ulysses S. Grant, would change his mind about parading through Richmond.

Grant was doing everything in his power to contain the crisis. He had rushed to Raleigh and helped Sherman revise the surrender terms, ignoring an order from Stanton to relieve him of command. Grant now suggested it might be a good idea for Sherman to march his army through Richmond, hoping it would remove the sting of Halleck's refusal to board them in the city. Sherman complied but warned Halleck to stay out of sight of his troops.

The Army of the Potomac spectators sneered at "Sherman's Greasers . . . dark with pitchpine smoke." For their part, the Westerners, having examined the city's defenses, said they could have taken Richmond in a week. Marching past Halleck's headquarters, one of Sherman's men broke ranks, sauntered up to the immaculate sentry at the door, and spit a stream of tobacco juice all over his polished shoes.

The nervous War Department ordered the Westerners to camp on the southern side of the

Potomac, hoping that a river between the two armies would reduce the friction. Sherman, however, refused; he stormed into the capital. Grant and Sherman's brother, Senator John Sherman of Ohio, calmed him down. Whether he could pacify his soldiers was not so certain.

Washington, still in mourning for the slain president, was draped in black. Nevertheless, the government launched an all-out effort to create a celebratory atmosphere. For five days before the march, workers decked every public building with blue-and-white bunting. Arches of spring flowers soared above Pennsylvania Avenue.

In front of the White House, carpenters hammered together a covered pavilion decorated with flags, flowers, and evergreens. The pavilion roof scrolled the names of the great Northern victories: Antietam, Gettysburg, Shiloh. Opposite this presidential reviewing stand was another covered platform for state governors, members of Congress, and Supreme Court justices. Other stands for guests, Army and Navy officers, the press, and convalescent soldiers stretched along both sides of the broad street.

Spectators surged into the capital from Maryland and more distant states. Henry Adams's future wife arrived with a group of young Massachusetts women to find every hotel and boardinghouse room in the city taken. They settled for a single attic room near The Willard Hotel. The day before the review, they hired carriages and rode out to the camps of the various Eastern regiments.

May 23, 1865, dawned hot and dry. Clouds of dust filled every street as chaises, carriages, and wagons lumbered toward Pennsylvania Avenue. The Army of the Potomac had the privilege of marching first. This was Washington's own army, the men who had defended the city from the Confederates in a score of desperate battles. At 9:00 a.m., a signal gun boomed, and the troops headed down the street. "The swaying of their bodies and the swinging of their arms were as measured as the vibrations of a pendulum," wrote one eyewitness. "Their muskets shone like a wall of steel."

Uniforms were spotless, shoes gleamed, and every man gripped his musket with a white-gloved hand. They came down the avenue in formation, twelve men to a file, while two bands, each the size of a symphony orchestra, played "When Johnnie Comes Marching Home," "Tramp Tramp Tramp, the Boys Are Marching," and "The Battle Hymn of the Republic."

At the head of the column rode the army's commander, Major General Meade, the hero of Gettysburg. Cheers rang out, and people pushed forward to place garlands around the neck of his horse. Meade, known to his men as Old Snapping Turtle, managed a frosty smile. He had had the difficult task of commanding this army in the shadow of Ulysses Grant, who was its real director in the convulsive, costly battles of 1864 that had loosened Robert E. Lee's grip on Richmond.

The crowd was baffled by Grant's absence. Grant could have led both armies. But he decided to let Meade and Sherman have the cheers. In the same simple uniform he had worn in the field, without a trace of gold braid, he had slipped through the White House grounds and taken his place on the reviewing stand.

The cavalry followed close behind Meade and his staff. Spectators searched in vain for another hero, Major General Philip Sheridan, who had led his cavalry on a scorched-earth campaign through the Shenandoah Valley; but he was on the Rio Grande warning the emperor Maximilian and his French backers to get out of Mexico. Even without Sheridan and his men, there was no less than seven miles of cavalry; it took the horsemen an hour to pass any point in the parade.

The star of the cavalry was Major General George Armstrong Custer. A *New York World* reporter noted his "sunrise of golden hair which ripples down upon his blue shoulders." Ignoring regulations as usual, Custer wore a crimson necktie and buckskin trousers. As he neared the reviewing stand, a woman rushed out of the crowd and threw a wreath of flowers to him. He lunged forward to catch it, and his horse bolted. Custer's hat blew off, and he went hurtling past the reviewing stand, hair streaming behind him "like the charge of a Sioux chieftain," one observer noted.

Next came some of the more colorful regiments of the Army of the Potomac: Zouaves in gaudy blue and red, Irish outfits with sprigs of green in their hats. Artillery gunners sat stiffly on caissons behind their weapons.

Battle flags - bullet-riddled, bloodstained, many in shreds - were hung with ribbons and garlands, and many people rushed into the street to press their lips against the torn folds.

It took seven hours for the Army of the Potomac to pass the reviewing stand. Even before the parade began, a reporter for *The New York Times*, which had been critical of Sherman's treaty with Johnston, presumed Meade's men would win the popularity contest. He predicted thin crowds for the next day's march. Most people would be "indifferent" about watching another column of men trudge past for seven or eight more hours in the hot sun.

Sherman thought the Easterners marched poorly - too many "turned their eyes around like country gawks to look at the big people on the stand" - and he scorned the "pampered and well-fed bands that are taught to play the latest operas." But to Meade, who eventually joined him on the reviewing stand, Sherman apologized in advance for his "poor tatterdemalion corps." Meade assured him the people would make allowances, and the bandmaster offered to bring his two regiments back for the Westerners. Sherman declined; he would depend on his regimental bands because the men were more used to marching with them.

The Army of the Tennessee had not done any parading for the better part of a year. Sherman summoned his top officers to a conference on the next day's march: "Be careful about your intervals and your tactics," he said. "I will give [the men] plenty of time to go to the Capitol and see everything afterward, but let them keep their eyes fifteen feet to the front and march by in the old customary way."

Major General William Hazen, thinking he was pleasing Sherman, asked his help to get the men of the XV Corps to cut their hair. Sherman refused, telling Hazen he wanted the spectators to see the army as it had looked on the march through the South.

At 9:00 a.m., the Army of the Tennessee rounded the corner of the Capitol and headed down Pennsylvania Avenue. The weather was not as warm as the day before. The number of spectators had grown. *The New York Times*'s reporter estimated the crowd at 200,000, noting that "thousands left the city after the first day but their places were taken by newcomers."

The pundits and politicians were finding out that however much they might deprecate Sherman and his soldiers, The Army of the Potomac had earned the people's admiration. But the Army of the Tennessee had an aura that compelled people to come see it.

"Uncle Billy" Sherman rode at the head of his troops, wreaths of roses around his horse's neck. His old slouch hat was in his hand, and his red hair glistened in the bright sun. Behind him, the plowboys from Ohio, Wisconsin, Illinois, and Michigan glanced, astonished, at the signs arched over the avenue: *HAIL TO THE WESTERN HEROES. HAIL, CHAMPIONS OF SHILOH, VICKSBURG, CHATTANOOGA, ATLANTA, SAVANNAH, PRIDE OF THE NATION.*

The Westerners were "nothing but bone and muscle and skin under their tattered battle-flags," said Brigadier General Carl Schurz, who marched with them. Another observer thought they marched "like the lords of the world." The *New York Tribune* reporter believed their faces were "more intelligent, self-reliant and determined" than those of the Army of the Potomac. The *New York World* declared them "hardier, knottier, weirder."

The Westerners were claiming their last victory.

The spectators went wild: Sobbing women held up babies; others praised God and wept. Rooftops, windows, even the trees were full of cheering civilians.

For some regiments, the excitement was almost unbearable. Wild cheers burst from their throats. Hearing those yells, Sherman rode in an agony of uncertainty. He could not break his own order and look back. He could only pray his legions had not become the undisciplined mob that the Army of the Potomac considered them. But as his bay horse mounted the slope before the Treasury Building, the general could stand the suspense no longer. Only minutes from the presidential reviewing stand, he whirled in his saddle.

What he saw made that "the happiest and most satisfactory moment" of his life. Even while cheering, every man stared rigidly ahead; all marched to the same beat. "The column was compact," he wrote in his memoirs, "and the glittering muskets looked like a solid mass of steel, moving with the regularity of a pendulum."

Sherman raised his sword in salute as he passed the presidential reviewing stand. The *New York World* reporter said the acclamation was "without precedent." Every man, woman, and child in the crowd shouted his lungs out "as if he had been the personal friend of each and every one of them." Sherman, the same man newspapers had called a traitor only ten days before, was "the idol of the day."

Regimental bands burst into "Marching through Georgia," and flowers poured down from the roofs and trees until the street was ankle-deep in blossoms. As the XV Corps passed the reviewing stand, the officers whipped off their hats and bellowed a cheer for the president, but their eyes remained locked to the front.

Sherman swung his horse into the White House grounds, dismounted, and joined the dignitaries on the reviewing stand. He embraced his wife and son for the first time in eighteen months and shook hands with his father-in-law, Thomas Ewing, Sr., Johnson, and Grant. When Stanton gamely put out his hand, Sherman ignored it, his face scarlet. "I declined it publicly," he wrote with grim satisfaction, "and the fact was universally noticed." Then he sat down to watch his men.

As the Army of the Tennessee continued its triumphant march along Pennsylvania Avenue, spectators were hypnotized by the accouterments the men had carried with them through the South. The *New York World* noted the sixteen-foot staffs with mysterious flags like "talismanic banners" hoisted by the signalmen. Nearly every company trailed behind it a captured horse or mule loaded with cooking utensils, chickens, and an occasional pig on a rope - explaining how they had marched through Georgia unsupplied except, in Grant's words, by "sweet potatoes sprung up from the ground."

Behind each division came living evidence of why they had fought - proof that the war had been, as Lincoln had hoped, "a new birth of freedom." A pioneer corps of black men marched in double ranks, with picks, staves, and axes slung across their shoulders. At the sight of six horse-drawn ambulances for each division - bloodstained stretchers strapped to their sides - a hush fell over the crowd.

On the reviewing stand, as the first divisions passed, the German ambassador said, "An army like that could whip all Europe." A half-hour later he gasped, "An army like that could whip the world." An hour later: "An army like that could whip the devil."

For seven and a half hours, the men of the West strode down Pennsylvania Avenue. By the end, the cheering spectators realized that the aura of invincibility came from something invisible, intangible, something profoundly connected to the idea of freedom. Lincoln had summoned these grandsons of the pioneers from the nation's heartland to settle the ancient issue between the founding sections. More than one spectator sensed it was the martyred president himself, in his Western prime, striding past them on May 24, 1865.

Within a month, this exotic host - and its less glamorous brothers in the Army of the Potomac - had vanished like its creator, "melted back," in the words of one newspaperman, "into the heart of the people from whence it came."

14

ASSASSINATION!

– PHILIP B. KUNHARDT JR.

At 10:30 p.m. on April 14, 1865, a man signaled with a lit candle from the stoop of Petersen's boardinghouse in Washington, D.C. and shouted, "Bring him in here!" In the street, twenty-five soldiers, doctors, and bystanders carried the body of Abraham Lincoln, sixteenth president of the United States and the first to be struck down by an assassin, out the doorway of Ford's Theater, heading to the nearest bed.

An officer's sword had opened a path in the crowd of onlookers, who stood transfixed with shock, eyes straining beyond the short flare of three gas jets to glimpse the familiar face. The president was naked to the waist; his overcoat, its collar sticky with blood, was flung over his chest.

The procession was halted twice while a surgeon plucked blood clots from the back of Lincoln's head, opening the wound so it could bleed freely. Whenever the bleeding stopped, so did the breathing, almost. At last, clumsily inching their way up the Peterson stoop and squeezing through the tight entrance, the bearers vanished from the crowd's view.

Abraham Lincoln had known he was in danger of being killed. By the beginning of his second term, the threats to his life had increased.

In 1861, Secretary of State William Henry Seward had declared confidently, "assassination is not an American habit or practice." By the end of the Civil War, he had changed his mind. After the Confederate surrender at Appomattox, Seward told Attorney General James Speed that some Southerners would be in a mood of absolute madness, and the president might indeed be killed. He advised Speed to go to City Point, Virginia, where Lincoln was visiting Ulysses S. Grant's army, and warn him to be careful.

When Speed arrived, Lincoln had already walked several miles through the still-burning city of Richmond. The city's white residents huddled inside their homes as a crowd of blacks followed Lincoln, trying to kneel in his path and bless him for their emancipation. The president made an easy target.

Lincoln later said it had occurred to him as he walked that a gun could have been aimed from any window along the route, but "I was not scared about myself one bit." He had the same feeling about his daily routine in Washington. "If anyone wanted to kill me," the president said, "he could shoot me from a window on Seventh Street any day when I am riding out to the Soldiers' Home [his summer residence]. I do not believe it is my fate to die in this way."

Speed tried to talk to Lincoln about Seward's fear, but "he stopped me at once, saying he had rather be dead than live in continual dread. Any precautions against assassination would be to him perpetual reminders of danger."

But Lincoln could not avoid the topic. When briefed by Secret Service detective La Fayette C. Baker on the latest threats, the president's manner became playful. "Well, Baker," he said, "what do they want to kill me for? If they kill me, they will run the risk of getting a worse man."

He also bantered with his friend and self-appointed bodyguard Ward Hill Lamon, who had gone to Richmond three days before the tragedy at Ford's Theater. Lamon tried to make Lincoln promise not to mingle with crowds, and especially not to go to the theater. Lincoln laughed and remarked to Secretary of the Interior John P. Usher, "this boy is a monomaniac on the subject of my safety."

But, sometimes suddenly, Lincoln would become depressed. "I shall never live out the four years of my term," he said. "When the rebellion is crushed, my work is done." In a cubbyhole of his office desk, Lincoln had eighty letters which he had tied together and labeled "Assassination." One letter instructed an anonymous assassin to get into "the monster's" office, "congratulate him, listen to his stories. . . . Abe must die and now. You can choose your weapons - the cup, the knife, the bullet."

Lincoln had already barely escaped a bullet. During the summer of 1864, as he entered the grounds of the Soldiers' Home, riding alone, a hidden marksman had fired at him, but the ball had whizzed through his high hat. He wanted the incident kept quiet, saying, "It was probably an accident and might worry my family."

There were rumors of other failed assassination attempts. Some said castor oil ordered from a pharmacy had arrived laced with poison. Another story was that a trunk of old clothes taken from yellow-fever victims in Cuba had been delivered to the White House in hopes of infecting the Lincolns with the deadly disease.

More than once, the same man warned Lincoln that a small, square package was being mailed that would explode when it was unwrapped. Lincoln told him each time, "No package yet, and I promise never to open any small square packages." Though the mail bomb never arrived, baskets of poisoned fruit occasionally did, and the president regularly received photographs and drawings of himself spattered with red ink.

Mary Todd Lincoln worried constantly over her husband's safety. To comfort her, he agreed to carry a sturdy cane. But, he often remarked, he would have had to shut himself up in an iron box to be really safe.

When Lincoln took the oath of office on March 4, 1861, he was the first American president to be sworn in under heavy military protection. Sharpshooters were stationed in every window of the two Capitol wings, with their guns trained on the small temporary platform on the steps of the east front. There had been a report that a bomb was set to go off under the platform, but a search revealed nothing.

Armed troops patrolled the side streets, according to the plan directed by "Old Fuss and Feathers" General Winfield Scott, who was a block away during the ceremony. Scott said he was determined that Lincoln would live to be inaugurated, and he considered this the most momentous hour of his career.

Cavalry officers who escorted Lincoln's carriage to the Capitol and later the White House were ordered to spur their animals with pretended clumsiness.

The plan was to create constant unpredictable movement so that any bullet fired at Lincoln would strike a horse instead.

Four years later, at the war's end, rumors persisted of a bomb that was ready to be fastened to crossbars under the presidential carriage - the same one in which Lincoln rode to Ford's Theater on the night he died. Still, nothing could spoil Lincoln's good mood that second week of April 1865.

General Robert E. Lee had surrendered at Appomattox on Palm Sunday, April 9. During the week that followed, Lincoln laughed as his son, Tad, waved a Rebel flag behind his back. He was the cordial host of White House dinner parties planned by the first lady. "I've never been so happy in my life," he declared.

Lincoln's happiness frightened Mary; the last time her husband had said, "I have never been so happy in my life," their three-year-old son Eddie had died the next day.

Mary had examined Bible verses read during her husband's second inauguration on March 4, and the words at the exact spot where he had kissed the page on taking the oath. The verse was in Isaiah 5; the prophet, speaking of the enemies of Israel, said, "None shall be weary nor stumble among them ... whose arrows are sharp, and all their bows bent, their horses' hoofs shall be counted like flint, and their wheels like a whirlwind." Mary believed it was a warning of danger, and that she must be on guard to protect the president.

An actor named John Wilkes Booth had been in the crowd for Lincoln's second inauguration - so close to the president, he later remarked, that he had an "excellent chance . . . to kill [him], if I had wished." Booth, a Confederate sympathizer from Maryland, had been plotting with others to kidnap Lincoln to leverage the release of Confederate prisoners of war. Later in March, the conspirators had surrounded and stopped a carriage, but Lincoln was not in it. By April, Booth had decided kidnapping would not do, that Lincoln must die. "Our country owed all her troubles to him, and God simply made me the instrument of His punishment," Booth wrote in his diary.

At 11:30 a.m. on April 14, a White House messenger arrived at Ford's Theater to report that Lincoln had accepted an invitation to that evening's performance of *Our American Cousin*. Theater manager John T. Ford had left his brother James in charge for the evening. James and another brother, Harry had prepared special seating for the president by combining boxes seven and eight, just over the stage at the right-hand side of the audience. The space was decorated with flags, a framed engraving of George Washington, and furnished with a sofa, two stuffed chairs on casters, and a rocking chair chosen specifically for Lincoln. Six straight-legged chairs were added for the president's guests.

Booth had been a regular player at Ford's Theater since 1864. Lincoln had attended a performance of *The Marble Heart*, in which Booth portrayed a Greek sculptor whose works came to life.

Booth was at the theater on the morning of April 14 when word arrived that Lincoln would be attending the play along with General Grant. He left the theater to begin a day of frenzied preparation to assassinate both Lincoln and Grant. Everyone who saw him from that moment on noticed he was deathly pale, and some thought he was sick.

That afternoon, Booth snuck back into the theater and rigged the door in the corridor leading to the president's box so it could be jammed shut. He either bored a peephole in the door to the box itself or possibly enlarged an existing one. Through it, he had a deadeye view of the back of the rocking chair where Lincoln would sit.

Captain Robert Todd Lincoln, the Lincolns' oldest son, had arrived home that morning. At breakfast, Robert was so sleepy he could barely keep his eyes open. After dinner, eager to sleep in a proper bed, he turned down his father's invitation to join him at the theater.

The Lincolns invited at least twelve others to the play, including Grant and his wife, Edwin Stanton,

Speaker of the House Schuyler Colfax, Illinois Governor Richard Oglesby, and Senator Richard Yates. Only two - Major Henry Reed Rathbone and his stepsister and fiancée, Clara Harris, daughter of a New York senator - accepted the invitation.

Walking to the War Department with his guard William Crook late that afternoon, Lincoln's mood swung suddenly. "Crook, do you know," he said, "I believe there are men who want to take my life." Then he lowered his voice, as though talking to himself. "And I have no doubt they will do it."

"Why do you think so, Mr. President?" asked Crook.

"Other men have been assassinated," Lincoln answered. "I know no one could do it and escape alive. But if it is to be done, it is impossible to prevent it."

Later, as Lincoln left for the theater, he said, "Goodby, Crook," instead of the usual "Good night."

At Pumphrey's Livery Stable, John Wilkes Booth hired a horse - a mare with a white star on her forehead. The stable owner warned him not to tie the mare if he left her; he must get someone to hold her because she was high-spirited and would break her halter. Booth mentioned he was going to Grover's Theater to write a letter, that he intended to stop for a drink somewhere, and then might take a pleasure ride.

Instead, Booth went to the National Hotel, where he was staying, to write his letter. He walked into the hotel office, seemingly looking for privacy. Dazed, he asked a clerk what year it was. Surely, the clerk said, he was joking; Booth said no, he wasn't.

At about 4:30 p.m., Booth met actor John Matthews, who was playing the part of an attorney in *Our American Cousin*. Booth handed Matthews the letter he had just written, and asked him to give it to the editor of the *National Intelligencer* the following day. Ten minutes later, Booth spotted the carriage taking Grant and his wife to a departing train and ran to peer into it, making its passengers uncomfortable.

At 6:30 p.m., Booth had dinner at the National Hotel. An hour later, he met his accomplices at the Herndon House and went over plans for them to kill Secretary of State Seward and Vice President Andrew Johnson. Since Grant wouldn't be at the theater, Booth dropped his plan for a second assassin in the box; he would act alone, with the help only of a stagehand to hold his horse.

The Lincolns picked up their guests at the Harris home, and they rode together to the theater. During the play, Mary laughed at every joke while her husband leaned forward and rested his chin in one hand, lost in thought.

At 9:30 p.m., Booth rode his horse into the alley

behind Ford's Theater. He gave the mare's bridle to a stagehand and entered the back door. Booth went under the stage and through a door to another alley that led to the front of the theater. Ticket seller John Buckingham saw Booth leave and enter the theater lobby five times.

Booth, nervous, asked Buckingham the time. Buckingham told him there was a clock in the lobby. It was after 10:00 p.m. When Buckingham went into the saloon next door for a drink, Booth was there drinking brandy. Fifteen minutes later, Booth stood in the back of the theater, looking at the audience. Then he walked up the stairs, humming a tune. A moment later, he entered the hall leading to the presidential box, wedged the door shut behind him so no one could follow, and drew his pistol. He opened the second door and stepped into the box directly behind President Lincoln.

Mary Lincoln later recalled that her hand was on her husband's knee. She was leaning across the arm of his chair, so close to him that she asked, with a look at the engaged couple in the front of the box, "What will Miss Harris think of my hanging on to you so?" The president's last words were, "She won't think anything about it."

On stage, the "American cousin" Asa, played by Harry Hawk, was rebuking the scheming English mother who had just found out he was not a rich catch for her daughter. "Don't know the manners of good society, eh? Well, I guess I know enough to turn you inside out, old gal. . ."

Lincoln was leaning forward, looking down into the audience, when Booth fired his derringer pistol just behind the president's head. The handmade lead bullet struck Lincoln behind the left ear, flattened out as it drove through his skull, tunneled into his brain, and stopped behind his right eye. Lincoln threw up his right arm, and Mary caught him around the neck, struggling to keep him upright.

A dense smoke enveloped the president and then curled upward, revealing the assassin. Rathbone lunged and grabbed at Booth's arm. Booth had dropped the single-shot pistol and was brandishing a dagger, which he tried to plunge into Rathbone's chest. The major knocked the knife upward and was cut deeply above the elbow. Booth leaped to the stage, twelve feet below. His right spur caught in the decorative bunting, and he landed heavily on his left leg, breaking his fibula. He hobbled across the stage, brandishing the dagger and shouting, "*Sic semper tyrannis!*"

The audience shouted, "Hang him!" In the box, Clara Harris screamed for water. Someone pounded on the corridor door that Booth had barred shut, and Rathbone, dripping blood from his arm, rushed to open it.

Dr. Charles Augustus Leale, coincidentally an avid student of gunshot wounds, had been seated in the dress circle forty feet from the president's box. He sat transfixed as Booth jumped to the stage. Then, gathering his wits, Leale hurdled over the seats; he got to the door just as it was being opened by Rathbone, who showed Leale his bleeding arm and begged for help. The doctor quickly saw the real help was needed by the president. "Oh, Doctor," Mary Lincoln cried, "do what you can for my dear husband! Is he dead? Can he recover?"

Lincoln was almost dead. He was paralyzed, with no pulse in his wrists, and if he was breathing, it was only at long intervals. Leale laid him on the floor, and with a penknife, cut his collar and coat around the shoulders and neck; having seen Booth's dagger and Rathbone's wound, he was looking for a knife slash. He ran his fingers through Lincoln's hair and removed a blood clot behind his left ear.

A second doctor, Charles Sabin Taft, bounded out of his seat in the orchestra, leapt onto the stage, and scrambled over the railing into the president's box. Leale straddled Lincoln's body, bent forward, opened his mouth, and pressed down the back of his tongue, which was blocking his windpipe. He directed Taft to raise and lower Lincoln's arms while he massaged the president's chest and silent heart. Lincoln took three gulps of air, then went still again.

Leale leaned down to seal his mouth against the president's, forcing air into the lungs. Lincoln started breathing on his own. Leale felt a faint, irregular flutter in the president's heart.

"His wound is mortal," Leale said. "We must get him to the nearest bed." Before the move was attempted, a diluted spoonful of brandy was poured between the president's lips. Lincoln had avoided alcohol all his life, saying it made him feel flabby and undone. He took three more sips of brandy before he died.

Laura Keene, the play's leading lady, arrived in the box with a pitcher of water and begged to be allowed to hold the president's head in her lap and bathe his temples. The actress sat on the floor, bending over Lincoln's upturned face as red stains spread on the skirt of her satin dress.

Two other doctors from the audience - Africanus F. A. King and Charles A. Gatch - helped Leale and Taft carry the president's body down the stairs, into the lobby of the theater, and out onto Tenth Street, where a path was being cleared by soldiers.

Henry Safford, who headed the War Department's property returns division, had been celebrating the war's end for five nights. That night, he had stayed home. He was jolted awake at about 10:30 p.m. as a mob poured from the theater doors. Safford threw open his window and shouted, "What's the matter?" Several yelled back at once: "The president has been shot!"

Safford lit a candle and ran down a narrow stairway to the front door of his boardinghouse, owned by a tailor named Peterson. He heard a voice asking, "Where shall we take him?"

Safford led the bearers to a small room at the end of the first-floor hall - a shed-like extension whose roof sloped from a high right-hand wall to a low window on the left. It was shabby, but there were clean sheets on the bed. William T. Clark, the young boarder whose modest room this was, took meticulous care of his few possessions.

The four doctors dismissed the other twenty-one bearers. Safford was sent to boil water and to search for bottles that could be filled and put next to the president's legs to warm him. The doctors stood helpless beside the bed, murmuring that they must let the president rest after the exertion of being carried across the street. Compelled to do something, they searched Lincoln's body for a stab wound but found none.

Mary Lincoln, escorted by Rathbone, appeared in the hallway, crying, "Where is my dear husband? Where is he?" She walked to the bed, where she saw him lying with his boots still on. The doctors asked her to leave while they made an examination, and she allowed herself to be led to a sitting room at the front of the house.

Rathbone unexpectedly was taking up most of the hallway space, extended full length on the floor and unconscious from loss of blood. The wound in his left arm had bled more as he was wrenched across the street by Mrs. Lincoln. Clara Harris arranged for a carriage to take her fiancee home.

Stanton had just begun to undress for bed when he heard a frantic shout that Secretary of State Seward had been murdered. Stanton rushed across Lafayette square to Seward's house, where the secretary of state lay unconscious but alive - his cheek and neck laid open by a deep knife wound inflicted by Booth's confederate Lewis Powell. Then Stanton learned of the attack on Lincoln and rushed to the house where the president was dying.

In all the confusion, Stanton took authority. He set up an office at the Petersen house, in the room next to where Lincoln lay, and with Assistant Secretary of War Charles Dana, began dictating orders and telegrams. The country had to be alerted, witnesses questioned, and the assassins identified and captured. Road blocks were to be set up in Maryland, the likely escape route to the South; all passenger trains and ships heading south on the Potomac were to be stopped; the sixty-eight forts and batteries guarding Washington were to be alerted; any suspicious persons in Alexandria were to be arrested. The order to all commanders: Find a man named John Wilkes Booth, "twenty-five years old [Booth was actually a month shy of twenty-seven], five feet eight inches tall, dark hair and mustache. Use all efforts to secure him."

As Lincoln lay dying, more than ninety people filed in and out of the small apartment. Sixteen doctors, including the Lincolns' family physician, tended to him. Members of his Cabinet rushed to his side from all over Washington.

Sumner, the abolitionist from Massachusetts, arrived with Robert Lincoln. Sitting down at the head of the deathbed, Sumner took the president's hand. A doctor said, "It's no use, Mr. Sumner. He can't hear you. He is dead."

"No, he isn't dead," replied Sumner. "Look at his face, he's breathing."

"It will never be anything more than this," the doctor said. Robert broke down in tears, and Sumner put his arm around the young man.

Secretary of the Navy Gideon Welles, when he learned of the assassination, remembered Lincoln telling him about a dream he'd had the night before of sailing in a strange vessel toward a shadowy shore. "Damn the Rebels," Welles said, shocking his wife who had never heard him swear, "this is their work!"

Stanton sent for Andrew Johnson, who had escaped harm when his designated assassin got drunk instead of carrying out his part in the plot. The vice president, Stanton thought, should make an appearance at the dying president's bedside. But Johnson had been there only a few minutes when word came from the front room that Mary Lincoln wanted to see her husband again. It was quickly agreed that Johnson must leave; the first lady despised him. The vice president went back to his hotel with a guard and spent the rest of the night excitedly pacing his room saying, "They shall suffer for this! They shall suffer for this!" Mary Lincoln never stopped believing Johnson was involved in the assassination plot. A year later, she wrote, "that miserable inebriate Johnson. He never wrote me a line of condolence and behaved in the most brutal way.... As sure as you and I live, Johnson had some hand in all this."

Dawn came. Doctor Africanus King noted at 6:25 a.m. that Lincoln's breaths were "jerking." At 6:40, his breathing was "prolonged and groaning - a deep, softly sonorous cooing sound at the end of each expiration." Then, "a minute without a breath, face growing dark." At 7:00, King wrote, "still breathing at long pauses."

Twenty-two minutes later, Taft's hand, pressed upon Abraham Lincoln's chest, felt the president's heart throb one last time and then go still. All night, Leale had held the president's hand "so that in his darkness he would know he had a friend."

Now the darkness was absolute. Edwin Stanton pronounced his famous benediction: "Now he belongs to the ages."

Later that morning, Mary Lincoln returned to the White House, but she refused to enter either her bedroom, in the southwest corner of the second floor, or her husband's, next to it. She settled for a room with no memories, which had served as the president's study. The shades were lowered, and the first lady collapsed into the bed, sobbing. Twelve-year-old Tad, who had run weeping to meet her as she got out of the carriage and buried his face in the folds of her dress, watched, terrified, as she convulsed with grief.

"Don't cry so, Mama, or you will make me cry too," Tad said, and Mary stopped; she could not bear to see Tad cry.

The news of the president's murder spread across the nation. Monday night, Lincoln was carried in a huge coffin downstairs to the East Room. On Tuesday, Lincoln belonged to the people. Early that morning, a line began forming outside the White House and was soon a mile long. At 9:30 a.m., the west driveway gate was opened, and the crowds silently filed in through the black-draped south portico.

In the center of the East Room stood a catafalque that reached as high as eleven feet from the floor. Eight tall mirrors over the eight marble mantelpieces were swathed from top to bottom with black cloth. Black streamers hung from the room's cornices. People walked past the coffin, pausing to look down at Lincoln's face. At 5:30 p.m., the public was shut out, and for the next two hours, privileged groups were admitted to the East Room.

At sunrise on Wednesday, April 19, Washington was awakened by the booming of cannons from forts encircling the city and the tolling bells in firehouses and church towers. The day was warm and cloudless - and as early as 8:00 a.m., throngs had gathered outside the White House and under the trees of Lafayette Square Park.

At 11:00 a.m., guests entered the East Room, now the funeral chamber, through the Green Room. The Blue Room, the adjoining oval parlor, was crowded with the late president's personal cavalry guard from Ohio, who had ridden their black horses wherever Lincoln went. The cavalrymen parted to allow a cortege that included General Grant to pass. At two minutes to noon, Andrew Johnson entered the chamber.

Honor guard officers stood at each corner of the catafalque. At the foot of the coffin sat Robert Lincoln, along with Ninian W. Edwards and Clark M. Smith of Springfield, the husbands of his mother's two sisters, and two of his mother's first cousins, Dr. Lyman Beecher Todd and General John B. S. Todd. Lincoln's two young secretaries, John Nicolay and John Hay, stood beside Robert. Mary Lincoln would have been at the foot of the coffin, too, had she been there at all. She remained upstairs in bed.

Grant, with tears in his eyes, sat alone at the president's head, facing a cross of lilies. Just a little over a year before, on March 8, 1864, he had paid his first visit to the White House after being made lieutenant general. It was the evening of a weekly reception, and Lincoln, surrounded by citizens in the oval Blue Room, spied the shy soldier and recognized him immediately from his photographs. The president stepped up the line to greet his new head of the armies, took hold of him and moved him along to Mrs. Lincoln, saying, "Here is General Grant. What a surprise! What a delight!"

Johnson stood at the east side of the coffin and behind him, the Cabinet. Just before the first of four ministers who were to conduct the service began speaking, Johnson and Preston King stepped up to the coffin, mounted the foot-high ledge at its side, looked down at Lincoln's face for a moment, then retired to their places a few feet back.

At 12:10 p.m., the service began. Bishop Simpson of the Methodist Episcopal Church delivered a prayer in which he likened Lincoln to Moses, who brought his people to the edge of the promised land but was not permitted to enter it. All 600 listeners were in tears.

Lincoln's pastor, Phineas Gurley, gave the funeral sermon, speaking of the "cruel, cruel hand, that dark hand of the assassin, which smote our honored, wise and noble president, and filled the land with sorrow."

Lincoln's old friend and bodyguard, Ward Hill Lamon, had made the arrangements for the great procession. Some of the units had been waiting for hours on side streets and joined the marching lines according to plan. Leading the procession, ahead of the coffin, was a detachment of black soldiers that had been the second to enter Richmond at its surrender. Officers of the Army, Navy, and Marine Corps followed. Then came the marshals, the clergymen who had conducted the funeral, the doctors who had attended the president on his deathbed, the twenty-two pallbearers, Grant, Admiral David Farragut, and finally the civilian mourners.

Lincoln's favorite horse, branded *U.S.*, trotted behind the hearse, his master's boots turned backward in the stirrups. Robert and Tad Lincoln rode in a carriage together, close enough to their father's body to see the continuous wave as men in the crowd removed hats by the hundreds as the coffin passed by.

Many convalescent soldiers had left their beds in

the Washington hospitals to march out of respect to their late commander in chief. Though some were too weak to go far, others hobbled on crutches all the way to the Capitol. The black citizens of Washington made one of the most impressive sights of all. They walked in lines of forty, straight across the avenue from curb to curb - 4,000 of them. They wore high silk hats and white gloves and marched in silence, holding hands.

Several weeks before this mournful day, the president and his wife were driving by horse and buggy along the James River in Virginia when they came to a country graveyard. It was far from the busy world and had tall trees, and on the graves, the buds of spring flowers were opening. They both wanted to stop and walk through it, and they did. Lincoln, said his wife, seemed thoughtful. He said, "Mary, you are younger than I. You will survive me. When I am gone, lay my remains in some quiet place like this."

Twenty days after the shooting at Ford's Theater, the president got his wish. After twelve funerals in twelve grieving cities as a special train carried him home to his prairie state, his coffin was placed in a hillside tomb in Oak Ridge Cemetery in Springfield, Illinois.

Made in the USA
Coppell, TX
30 June 2021

58355343R10193